FOREWORD

The collection of "Everything Will Be Okay" travel phrasebooks published by T&P Books is designed for people traveling abroad for tourism and business. The phrasebooks contain what matters most - the essentials for basic communication. This is an indispensable set of phrases to "survive" while abroad.

This phrasebook will help you in most cases where you need to ask something, get directions, find out how much something costs, etc. It can also resolve difficult communication situations where gestures just won't help.

This book contains a lot of phrases that have been grouped according to the most relevant topics. A separate section of the book also provides a small dictionary with more than 1,500 important and useful words.

Take "Everything Will Be Okay" phrasebook with you on the road and you'll have an irreplaceable traveling companion who will help you find your way out of any situation and teach you to not fear speaking with foreigners.

TABLE OF CONTENTS

T&P Books Publishing

Travel phrasebooks collection
«Everything Will Be Okay!»

T&P Books Publishing

PHRASEBOOK

— PERSIAN —

THE MOST IMPORTANT PHRASES

This phrasebook contains
the most important
phrases and questions
for basic communication
Everything you need
to survive overseas

T&P BOOKS

By Andrey Taranov

Phrasebook + 1500-word dictionary

English-Persian phrasebook & concise dictionary

By Andrey Taranov

The collection of "Everything Will Be Okay" travel phrasebooks published by T&P Books is designed for people traveling abroad for tourism and business. The phrasebooks contain what matters most - the essentials for basic communication. This is an indispensable set of phrases to "survive" while abroad.

Another section of the book also provides a small dictionary with more than 1,500 useful words arranged alphabetically. The dictionary includes a lot of gastronomic terms and will be helpful when ordering food at a restaurant or buying groceries at the store.

T&P Books Publishing
www.tpbooks.com

ISBN: 978-1-78716-926-5

This book is also available in E-book formats.
Please visit www.tpbooks.com or the major online bookstores.

PRONUNCIATION

T&P phonetic alphabet	Persian example	English example
['] (ayn)	دعوا [da'vā]	voiced pharyngeal fricative
['] (hamza)	تایید [ta'id]	glottal stop
[a]	رود [ravad]	shorter than in ask
[ā]	آتش [ātaš]	calf, palm
[b]	بانک [bānk]	baby, book
[č]	چند [čand]	church, French
[d]	هشتاد [haštād]	day, doctor
[e]	عشق [ešq]	elm, medal
[f]	فندک [fandak]	face, food
[g]	لوگو [logo]	game, gold
[h]	گیاه [giyāh]	home, have
[i]	جزیره [jazire]	shorter than in feet
[j]	جشن [jašn]	joke, general
[k]	کاج [kāj]	clock, kiss
[l]	لیمو [limu]	lace, people
[m]	ماجرا [mājarā]	magic, milk
[n]	نروژ [norvež]	sang, thing
[o]	گلف [golf]	pod, John
[p]	اپرا [operā]	pencil, private
[q]	لاغر [lāqar]	between [g] and [h]
[r]	رقم [raqam]	rice, radio
[s]	سوپ [sup]	city, boss
[š]	دوش [duš]	machine, shark
[t]	ترجمه [tarjome]	tourist, trip
[u]	نیرو [niru]	book
[v]	ورشو [varšow]	very, river
[w]	روشن [rowšan]	vase, winter
[x]	کاخ [kāx]	as in Scots 'loch'
[y]	بیابان [biyābān]	yes, New York
[z]	زنجیر [zanjir]	zebra, please
[ž]	ژوئن [žuan]	forge, pleasure

LIST OF ABBREVIATIONS

English abbreviations

ab.	-	about
adj	-	adjective
adv	-	adverb
anim.	-	animate
as adj	-	attributive noun used as adjective
e.g.	-	for example
etc.	-	et cetera
fam.	-	familiar
fem.	-	feminine
form.	-	formal
inanim.	-	inanimate
masc.	-	masculine
math	-	mathematics
mil.	-	military
n	-	noun
pl	-	plural
pron.	-	pronoun
sb	-	somebody
sing.	-	singular
sth	-	something
v aux	-	auxiliary verb
vi	-	intransitive verb
vi, vt	-	intransitive, transitive verb
vt	-	transitive verb

PERSIAN PHRASEBOOK

This section contains
important phrases that may
come in handy in various
real-life situations.
The phrasebook will help
you ask for directions, clarify
a price, buy tickets, and
order food at a restaurant

T&P Books Publishing

PHRASEBOOK
CONTENTS

T&P Books Publishing

The bare minimum

Excuse me, ...
bebaxšid, ...
ببخشید، ....

Hello.
salãm
سلام.

Thank you.
mamnun
ممنون

Good bye.
xodãhãfez
خداحافظ.

Yes.
bale
بله

No.
xeyr
خیر

I don't know.
nemidãnam
نمی دانم.

Where? | Where to? | When?
kojã? | kojã? | key?
کی؟ | کجا؟ | کجا؟

I need ...
be ... ehtiyãj dãram
به...أحتیاج دارم

I want ...
mixãham ...
می خواهم...

Do you have ...?
ãyã ... dãrid?
آیا...دارید؟

Is there a ... here?
ãyã injã ... hast?
آیا اینجا ...هست؟

May I ...?
mitavãnam ...?
می توانم...؟

..., please (polite request)
lotfan
لطفاً

I'm looking for ...
donbãl-e ... migardam
دنبال...می گردم.

restroom
tuãlet
توالت

ATM
xodpardãz
خودپرداز

pharmacy (drugstore)
dãruxãne
داروخانه

hospital
bimãrestãn
بیمارستان

police station
edãre-ye polis
اداره پلیس

subway
istgãh-e metro
ایستگاه مترو

taxi	tāksi
	تاکسی
train station	istgāh-e qatār
	ایستگاه قطار

My name is ...	esm-e man ... ast
	اسم من...است.
What's your name?	esm-e šomā čist?
	اسم شما چیست؟
Could you please help me?	lotfan mitavānid komakam konid?
	لطفاً می توانید کمکم کنید؟
I've got a problem.	yek moškel dāram
	یک مشکل دارم.
I don't feel well.	hālam xub nist
	حالم خوب نیست.
Call an ambulance!	āmbulāns xabar konid!
	آمبولانس خبر کنید!
May I make a call?	mitavānam yek telefon bezanam?
	می توانم یک تلفن بزنم؟

I'm sorry.	ma'zerat mixāham
	معذرت می خواهم.
You're welcome.	xāheš mikonam
	خواهش می کنم.

I, me	man
	من
you (inform.)	to
	تو
he	u
	او
she	u
	او
they (masc.)	an-hā
	آنها
they (fem.)	an-hā
	آنها
we	mā
	ما
you (pl)	šomā
	شما
you (sg, form.)	šomā
	شما

ENTRANCE	vorudi
	ورودی
EXIT	xoruji
	خروجی
OUT OF ORDER	xarāb
	خراب
CLOSED	baste
	بسته

OPEN	bāz
	باز
FOR WOMEN	zanāne
	زنانه
FOR MEN	mardāne
	مردانه

Questions

Where?	kojā? کجا؟
Where to?	kojā? کجا؟
Where from?	az kojā? از کجا؟
Why?	čerā? چرا؟
For what reason?	be če dalil? به چه دلیل؟
When?	key? کی؟
How long?	če modat? چه مدت؟
At what time?	če sāati? چه ساعتی؟
How much?	čand ast? چنداست؟
Do you have ...?	āyā ... dārid? آیا ...دارید؟
Where is ...?	... kojāst? ...کجاست؟
What time is it?	sāat čand ast? ساعت چند است؟
May I make a call?	mitavānam yek telefon bezanam? می توانم یک تلفن بزنم؟
Who's there?	kiye? کیه؟
Can I smoke here?	mitavānam injā sigār bekešam? می توانم اینجا سیگار بکشم؟
May I ...?	mitavānam ...? می توانم...؟

Needs

I'd like ...	mixāham ... می خواهم...
I don't want ...	nemixāham ... نمی خواهم...
I'm thirsty.	tešne hastam تشنه هستم.
I want to sleep.	mixāham bexābam می خواهم بخوابم.
I want ...	mixāham ... می خواهم...
to wash up	xod rā bešuyam خود را بشویم
to brush my teeth	dandānhāyam rā mesvāk bezanam دندان هایم را مسواک بزنم
to rest a while	kami esterāhat konam کمی استراحت کنم
to change my clothes	lebashāyam rā avaz konam لباسهایم را عوض کنم
to go back to the hotel	be hotel bargaštan به هتل برگشتن
to buy ...	... xaridan ...خریدن
to go to ...	be ... raftan به...رفتن
to visit ...	az ... bāzdid kardan از...بازدید کردن
to meet with ...	bā ... molāqāt kardan با...ملاقات کردن
to make a call	telefon zadan تلفن زدن
I'm tired.	xaste-am خسته ام.
We are tired.	xaste-im خسته ایم.
I'm cold.	sardam ast سردم است.
I'm hot.	garmam ast گردم است.
I'm OK.	xub hastam خوب هستم.

I need to make a call.

niyāz dāram telefon bezanam

نیازدارم تلفن بزنم.

I need to go to the restroom.

bayad be tuālet beravam

باید به توالت بروم.

I have to go.

bāyad beravam

باید بروم.

I have to go now.

bāyad alān beravam

باید الان بروم.

Asking for directions

Excuse me, ...	bebaxšid, ... ببخشید،...
Where is ...?	... kojāst? ...کجاست؟
Which way is ...?	... az kodām taraf ast? ...از کدام طرف است؟
Could you help me, please?	mitavānid lotfan komakam konid? می توانید لطفاً کمکم کنید؟

I'm looking for ...	donbāl-e ... migardam دنبال...می گردم
I'm looking for the exit.	donbāl-e xoruji migardam دنبال خروجی می گردم.
I'm going to ...	be ... miravam به...می روم
Am I going the right way to ...?	in rāh barāye raftan be ... dorost ast? این راه برای رفتن به...درست است؟

Is it far?	dur ast? دور است؟
Can I get there on foot?	mitavānam piyāde beravam? می توانم پیاده بروم؟
Can you show me on the map?	mitavānid ruye naqše nešānam bedahid? می توانید روی نقشه نشانم بدهید؟
Show me where we are right now.	lotfan be man nešān bedahid alān kojā hastim لطفاً به من نشان بدهید الان کجا هستیم.

Here	injā اینجا
There	ānjā آنجا
This way	az in rāh از این راه

Turn right.	dast-e rast bepičid دست راست بپیچید.
Turn left.	dast-e čap bepičid دست چپ بپیچید.
first (second, third) turn	be avvalin (dovvomin, sevvomin) xiyābān bepičid. به اولین(دومین، سومین)خیابان بپیچید.

to the right	dast-e rāst
	دست راست
to the left	dast-e čap
	دست چپ
Go straight ahead.	mostaqim beravid
	مستقیم بروید.

Signs

WELCOME!	xoš āmadid خوش آمدید
ENTRANCE	vorudi ورودی
EXIT	xoruji خروجی
PUSH	fešār bedahid فشار بدهید
PULL	bekešid بکشید
OPEN	bāz باز
CLOSED	baste بسته
FOR WOMEN	zanāne زنانه
FOR MEN	mardāne مردانه
GENTLEMEN, GENTS (m)	āqāyān آقایان
WOMEN (f)	xānomha خانمها
DISCOUNTS	taxfif تخفیف
SALE	harāj حراج
FREE	rāygān رایگان
NEW!	jadid جدید
ATTENTION!	movāzeb bāšid مواظب باشید
NO VACANCIES	zarfiyat takmil ظرفیت تکمیل
RESERVED	rezerv šode رزرو شده
ADMINISTRATION	edāre اداره
STAFF ONLY	moxtas-e kārkonān مختص کارکنان

BEWARE OF THE DOG!	movāzeb-e sag bāšid
	مواظب سگ باشید
NO SMOKING!	sigār nakešid
	سیگار نکشید
DO NOT TOUCH!	dast nazanid
	دست نزنید
DANGEROUS	xatarnāk
	خطرناک
DANGER	xatar
	خطر
HIGH VOLTAGE	voltāj-e bālā
	ولتاژ بالا
NO SWIMMING!	šenā mamnu'
	شنا ممنوع

OUT OF ORDER	xarāb
	خراب
FLAMMABLE	qābel-e ešteāl
	قابل اشتعال
FORBIDDEN	mamnu'
	ممنوع
NO TRESPASSING!	vorud mamnu'
	ورود ممنوع
WET PAINT	rang-e xis
	رنگ خیس

CLOSED FOR RENOVATIONS	barāye ta'mirāt baste ast
	برای تعمیرات بسته است
WORKS AHEAD	dar dast-e ta'mir
	در دست تعمیر
DETOUR	masir-e enherāfi
	مسیرانحرافی

Transportation. General phrases

plane	havāpeymā
	هواپیما
train	qatār
	قطار
bus	otobus
	اتوبوس
ferry	kašti
	کشتی
taxi	tāksi
	تاکسی
car	māšin
	ماشین
schedule	jadval-e sāāt
	جدول ساعات
Where can I see the schedule?	jadval-e sāāt rā kojā mtavānam bebinam?
	جدول ساعات را کجا می توانم ببینم؟
workdays (weekdays)	ruzhā-ye bāz
	روزهای باز
weekends	ruzhā-ye baste
	روزهای بسته
holidays	ruzhā-ye ta'til
	روزهای تعطیل
DEPARTURE	harekat
	حرکت
ARRIVAL	vorud
	ورود
DELAYED	bā ta'xir
	باتاخیر
CANCELLED	kansel šode
	کنسل شده
next (train, etc.)	ba'di
	بعدی
first	avvalin
	اولین
last	āxarin
	آخرین

When is the next ...?	... ba'di če sāati ast?
	...بعدی چه ساعتی است؟
When is the first ...?	avvalin ... če sāati ast?
	اولین... چه ساعتی است؟
When is the last ...?	āxarin ... če sāati ast?
	آخرین... چه ساعتی است؟

transfer (change of trains, etc.)	terānsfer
	ترانسفر
to make a transfer	terānsfer gereftan
	ترانسفر گرفتن
Do I need to make a transfer?	āyā bāyad terānsfer begiram?
	آیا باید ترانسفر بگیرم؟

Buying tickets

Where can I buy tickets?	kojā mitavānam bilit bexaram? کجامی توانم بلیط بخرم؟
ticket	bilit بلیط
to buy a ticket	ilit xaridan بلیط خریدن
ticket price	qeymat-e yek bilit قیمت یک بلیط
Where to?	barāye kojā? برای کجا؟
To what station?	če maqsadi? چه مقصدی؟
I need ...	be ... niyāz dāram به...نیازدارم
one ticket	yek bilit یک بلیط
two tickets	do bilit دو بلیط
three tickets	se bilit سه بلیط
one-way	raft رفت
round-trip	rafo-o-bargašt رفت و برگشت
first class	daraje yek درجه یک
second class	daraje do درجه دو
today	emruz امروز
tomorrow	fardā فردا
the day after tomorrow	pas fardā پس فردا
in the morning	sobh صبح
in the afternoon	ba'd az zohr بعد از ظهر
in the evening	šab شب

aisle seat

sandali-ye taraf-e rāhro

صندلی طرف راهرو

window seat

sandali-ye taraf-e panjare

صندلی طرف پنجره

How much?

čand ast?

چنداست؟

Can I pay by credit card?

mitavānam bā kārt bepardāzam?

می توانم با کارت بپردازم؟

Bus

bus	otobus اتوبوس
intercity bus	otobus-e beyn-e šahri اتوبوس بین شهری
bus stop	istgāh-e otobus ایستگاه اتوبوس
Where's the nearest bus stop?	nazdiktarin istgāh-e otobus kojāst? نزدیکترین ایستگاه اتوبوس کجاست؟
number (bus ~, etc.)	šomāre شماره (اتوبوس، غیره)
Which bus do I take to get to ...?	barāye raftan be ... če otobusi rā bāyad begiram? برای رفتن به...چه اتوبوسی را باید بگیرم؟
Does this bus go to ...?	āyā in otobus be ... miravad? آیا این اتوبوس به...می رود؟
How frequent are the buses?	otobus har čand vaqt yekbār rāh mioftad? اتوبوس هر چند وقت یکبار راه می افتد؟
every 15 minutes	har pānzdah daqiqe yekbār هر 15 دقیقه یکبار
every half hour	har nim sāat yekbār هر نیم ساعت یکبار
every hour	har sāat هر ساعت
several times a day	čand bār dar ruz چند بار در روز
... times a day	... bār dar ruz ...بار در روز
schedule	jadval-e sāāt جدول ساعات
Where can I see the schedule?	jadval-e sāāt rā kojā mtavānam bebinam? جدول ساعات را کجا می توانم ببینم؟
When is the next bus?	otobus-e ba'di če sāati ast? اتوبوس بعدی چه ساعتی است؟
When is the first bus?	otobus-e avval če sāati ast? اتوبوس اول چه ساعتی است؟
When is the last bus?	otobus-e axar če sāati ast? اتوبوس آخر چه ساعتی است؟

stop	istgāh
	ایستگاه
next stop	istgāh-e ba'di
	ایستگاه بعدی
last stop (terminus)	termināl
	ترمینال
Stop here, please.	lotfan injā tavaqqof konid
	لطفاً اینجا توقف کنید.
Excuse me, this is my stop.	bebaxšid, istgāh-e man injāst
	ببخشید، ایستگاه من اینجاست.

Train

train	qatār قطار
suburban train	qatār-e beyn-e šahri قطار بیرون شهری
long-distance train	qatār-e safari قطار سفری
train station	istgāh-e qatar ایستگاه قطار
Excuse me, where is the exit to the platform?	bebaxšid, xoruji be samt-e sakuhā kojāst? ببخشید، خروجی به سمت سکوها کجاست؟
Does this train go to …?	āyā in qatār be … miravad? آیا این قطار به...می رود؟
next train	qatār-e ba'di قطار بعدی
When is the next train?	qatār-e ba'di če sāati ast? قطار بعدی چه ساعتی است؟
Where can I see the schedule?	jadval-e sāāt rā kojā mtavānam bebinam? جدول ساعات را کجا می توانم ببینم؟
From which platform?	az kodām sakku? از کدام سکو؟
When does the train arrive in …?	če sāati qatār be … miresad? چه ساعتی قطار به... می رسد؟
Please help me.	lotfan be man komak konid لطفاً به من کمک کنید.
I'm looking for my seat.	donbāl-e jā-ye xod migardam دنبال جای خود می گردم.
We're looking for our seats.	donbāl-e jā-hāye xod migardim دنبال جاهای خود می گردیم.
My seat is taken.	jā-ye man gerefte šode ast جای من گرفته شده است.
Our seats are taken.	jā-hāye mā gerefte šode and جاهای ما گرفته شده اند.
I'm sorry but this is my seat.	bebaxšid, injā jā-ye man ast ببخشید، اینجا جای من است.

Is this seat taken?   āyā in jā āzād ast?
آیا این جا آزاد است؟

May I sit here?   mitavānam injā benešinam?
می توانم اینجا بنشینم؟

On the train. Dialogue (No ticket)

Ticket, please.
bilit, lotfan
بلیط، لطفاً.

I don't have a ticket.
bilit nadāram
بلیط ندارم.

I lost my ticket.
bilitam rā gom kardeam
بلیطم را گم کرده ام.

I forgot my ticket at home.
bilitam rā dar xāne jā gozāšteam
بلیطم را در خانه جا گذاشته ام.

You can buy a ticket from me.
mitavanid bilit rā az man bexarid
می توانید بلیط را از من بخرید.

You will also have to pay a fine.
bāyad jarime-i rā ham bepardāzid
باید جریمه ای را هم بپردازید.

Okay.
bāšad
باشد.

Where are you going?
kojā miravid?
کجا می روید؟

I'm going to ...
be ... miravam
به...می روم.

How much? I don't understand.
čeqadr? motevajeh našodam
چقدر؟ متوجه نشدم.

Write it down, please.
lotfan ānrā benevisid
لطفاً آنرا بنویسید.

Okay. Can I pay with a credit card?
bale. mitavānam bā kārt bepardāzam?
بله. می توانم با کارت بپردازم؟

Yes, you can.
bale, hatman
بله، حتماً.

Here's your receipt.
in resid-e šomāst
این رسید شماست.

Sorry about the fine.
bābat-e jarime moteasefam
بابت جریمه متاسفم.

That's okay. It was my fault.
moškeli nist. taqsir-e xod-e man ast
مشکلی نیست. تقصیر خود من است.

Enjoy your trip.
safar bexeyr
سفر بخیر.

Taxi

taxi	tāksi تاکسی
taxi driver	rānande tāksi راننده تاکسی
to catch a taxi	tāksi gereftan تاکسی گرفتن
taxi stand	istgāh-e tāksi ایستگاه تاکسی
Where can I get a taxi?	kojā mitavānam tāksi begiram? کجا می توانم تاکسی بگیرم؟
to call a taxi	tāksi sedā zadan تاکسی صدا زدن
I need a taxi.	tāksi lāzem dāram تاکسی لازم دارم.
Right now.	alān الان
What is your address (location)?	ādres-e šomā kojāst? آدرس شما کجاست؟
My address is ...	ādres-e man ... ast. آدرس من...است.
Your destination?	maqsad-e šoma? مقصد شما؟
Excuse me, ...	bebaxšid, ...،ببخشید
Are you available?	āzād hastid? آزاد هستید؟
How much is it to get to ...?	hazine-ye raftan be ... čeqadr mišavad? هزینه رفتن به...چقدر می شود؟
Do you know where it is?	midānid kojāst? می دانید کجاست؟
Airport, please.	forudgāh, lotfan فرودگاه، لطفاً.
Stop here, please.	lotfan injā tavaqqof konid لطفاً اینجا توقف کنید.
It's not here.	injā nist اینجا نیست.
This is the wrong address.	ādres eštebāh ast آدرس اشتباه است.
Turn left.	dast-e čap bepičid دست چپ بپیچید.
Turn right.	dast-e rast bepičid دست راست بپیچید.

How much do I owe you?	čeqadr be šomā bepardāzam? چقدر به شما بپردازم؟
I'd like a receipt, please.	lotfan yek resid be man bedahid لطفاً یک رسیدبه من بدهید.
Keep the change.	bagiye-ye pul rā negah dārid بقیه پول را نگه دارید.

Would you please wait for me?	lotfan mitavānid montazer-e man bemānid? لطفاً می توانید منتظر من بمانید؟

five minutes	panj daqiqe پنج دقیقه
ten minutes	dah daqiqe ده دقیقه
fifteen minutes	pānzdah daqiqe پانزده دقیقه
twenty minutes	bist daqiqe بیست دقیقه
half an hour	nim sāat نیم ساعت

Hotel

Hello.	salām
	سلام.
My name is ...	esm-e man ... ast
	اسم من...است.
I have a reservation.	yek otāq rezerv kardeam
	یک اتاق رزرو کرده ام.
I need ...	be ... niyāz dāram
	به...نیازدارم
a single room	yek otāq-e yek nafare
	یک اتاق یک نفره
a double room	yek otāq-e do nafare
	یک اتاق دو نفره
How much is that?	qeymat-e ān čand ast?
	قیمت آن چند است؟
That's a bit expensive.	kami gerān ast
	کمی گران است.
Do you have anything else?	gozine-ye digari ham dārid?
	گزینه دیگری هم دارید؟
I'll take it.	ān rā rā migiram
	آن را را می گیرم.
I'll pay in cash.	naaqdi pardāxt mikonam
	نقدی پرداخت می کنم.
I've got a problem.	yek moškel dāram
	یک مشکل دارم.
My ... is broken.	...man šekaste ast
	... من شکسته است.
My ... is out of order.	...man kār nemikonad
	...من کار نمی کند.
TV	televiziyon
	تلویزیون
air conditioner	tahviye-ye matbuʿ
	تهویه مطبوع
tap	šir-e āb
	شیر آب
shower	duš
	دوش
sink	sink
	سینک
safe	gāv sandoq
	گاو صندوق

door lock	qofl-e dar
	قفل در
electrical outlet	piriz-e barq
	پریز برق
hairdryer	sešoār
	سشوار

I don't have ...	... nadāram.
	...ندارم.
water	āb
	آب
light	nur
	نور
electricity	barq
	برق

Can you give me ...?	mitavānid ... be man bedahid?
	می توانید... به من بدهید؟
a towel	yek hole
	یک حوله
a blanket	yek patu
	یک پتو
slippers	dampāyi
	دمپایی
a robe	yek robdošāmbr
	یک روب دوشامبر
shampoo	šāmpo
	شامپو
soap	sabun
	صابون

I'd like to change rooms.	mixāham otāqam rā avaz konam
	می خواهم اتاقم را عوض کنم.
I can't find my key.	kelidam rā peydā nemikonam
	کلیدم را پیدا نمی کنم.
Could you open my room, please?	mitavānid lotfan otāqam rā bāz konid?
	می توانید لطفأ اتاقم را باز کنید؟
Who's there?	kiye?
	کیه؟
Come in!	befarmāyid tu!
	!بفرمایید تو
Just a minute!	yek lahze!
	!یک لحظه
Not right now, please.	lotfan alān na
	لطفأ الان نه.

Come to my room, please.	mitavānid lotfan be otāq-e man biyāyid?
	می توانید لطفأ به اتاق من بیایید؟
I'd like to order food service.	mixāham qazāye dāxel-e otāq
	rā sefāres bedaham
	می خواهم غذای داخل اتاق راسفارش بدهم.

My room number is ...

šomāre-ye otāq-e man ... ast

شماره اتاق من... است.

I'm leaving ...

man ... miravam

من...می روم

We're leaving ...

mā ... miravim

ما...می رویم

right now

alān

الان

this afternoon

emruz ba'd az zohr

امروز بعد از ظهر

tonight

emšab

امشب

tomorrow

fardā

فردا

tomorrow morning

fardā sobh

فردا صبح

tomorrow evening

fardā ba'd az zohr

فردا بعد از ظهر

the day after tomorrow

pas fardā

پس فردا

I'd like to pay.

mixāham hesāb-e xod ra bepardāzam

می خواهم حساب خود را بپردازم.

Everything was wonderful.

hame čiz xeyli āli bud

همه چیز خیلی عالی بود.

Where can I get a taxi?

kojā mitavānam tāksi begiram?

کجا می توانم تاکسی بگیرم؟

Would you call a taxi for me, please?

mitavānid lotfan yek tāksi barāyam
sedā konid?

می توانید لطفاً یک تاکسی برایم صدا کنید؟

Restaurant

Can I look at the menu, please?	mitavānam lotfan meno rā bebinam? می توانم لطفاً منو را ببینم؟
Table for one.	yek miz-e yek nafare یک میز یک نفره.
There are two (three, four) of us.	do (se, čāhār) nafar hastim دو (سه، چهار) نفر هستیم.

Smoking	sigāri سیگاری
No smoking	qeyre sigāri غیر سیگاری
Excuse me! (addressing a waiter)	bebaxšid! ببخشید!
menu	meno منو
wine list	meno-ye mašrubāt منوی مشروبات
The menu, please.	meno lotfan منو، لطفاً.

Are you ready to order?	mixāhid sefārešetān rā bedahid? می خواهید سفارشتان رابدهید؟
What will you have?	če meyl mikonid? چه میل می کنید؟
I'll have ...	yek ... migiram یک...می گیرم

I'm a vegetarian.	giyāhxār hastam گیاهخوار هستم.
meat	gušt گوشت
fish	māhi ماهی
vegetables	sabzijāt سبزیجات
Do you have vegetarian dishes?	qāzāhā-ye giyāhi dārid? غذاهای گیاهی دارید؟
I don't eat pork.	gušt-e xuk nemixoram گوشت خوک نمی خورم.
He /she/ doesn't eat meat.	u gušt nemixorad او گوشت نمی خورد.
I am allergic to ...	be ... hassāsiyat dāram به...حساسیت دارم

Would you please bring me ...	mitavānid lotfa ... barāyam biyāvarid
	می توانیدلطفاً...برایم بیاورید.
salt | pepper | sugar	namak | felfel | šekar
	شکرا فلفل انمک
coffee | tea | dessert	qahve | čāy | deser
	دسر ا چای ا قهوه
water | sparkling | plain	āb | gāzdār | bigāz
	بی گاز ا گازدار ا آب
a spoon | fork | knife	yek qāšoq | yek čangāl | yek kārd
	یک کارد ا یک چنگال ا یک قاشق
a plate | napkin	yek bošqāb | yek dastmāl
	یک دستمال ا یک بشقاب

Enjoy your meal!	meyl befarmāyid!
	میل بفرمایید!
One more, please.	yeki digar lotfan
	یکی دیگر لطفاً.
It was very delicious.	besyār xošmaze bud
	بسیار خوشمزه بود.

check | change | tip	surat hesāb | pul-e xord | an'ām
	انعام ا پول خرد ا صورت حساب
Check, please.	surat hesab, lotfan
(Could I have the check, please?)	صورت حساب لطفاً.
Can I pay by credit card?	mitavānam bā kārt bepardāzam?
	می توانم با کارت بپردازم؟
I'm sorry, there's a mistake here.	bebaxšid, fekr mikonam injā eštebāhi sode ast
	ببخشید، فکرمی کنم اینجا اشتباهی شده است.

Shopping

Can I help you?
mitavānam komaketān konam?
می توانم کمکتان کنم؟

Do you have ...?
āyā ... dārid?
آیا...دارید؟

I'm looking for ...
donbāl-e ... migardam
دنبال...می گردم

I need ...
be ... ehtiyāj dāram
به...احتیاج دارم

I'm just looking.
faqat negāh mikonam mamnun
فقط نگاه می کنم، ممنون.

We're just looking.
faqat negāh mikonim, mamnun
فقط نگاه می کنیم، ممنون.

I'll come back later.
yek bār-e digar xāham āmad
یک بار دیگر خواهم آمد.

We'll come back later.
yek bār-e digar xāhim āmad
یک بار دیگر خواهیم آمد.

discounts | sale
taxfif | harāj
حراج | تخفیف

Would you please show me ...
mitavānid lotfan ... rā be man nešān bedahid
می توانید لطفاً ... را به من نشان بدهید؟

Would you please give me ...
lotfan ... rā be man bedahid
لطفاً...را به من بدهید

Can I try it on?
mitavānam in rā emtehān konam?
می توانم این را امتحان کنم؟

Excuse me, where's the fitting room?
bebaxšid, kabin-e porov kojāst?
ببخشید، کابین پرو کجاست؟

Which color would you like?
če rangi rā dust dā rid?
چه رنگی را دوست دارید؟

size | length
sā yz | bolandi
بلندی | سایز

How does it fit?
āyā sāyz-e šomā mibāšad?
آیا سایز شما می باشد؟

How much is it?
qeymat-e ān čand ast?
قیمت آن چند است؟

That's too expensive.
xeyli gerān ast
خیلی گران است.

I'll take it.
ān rā rā migiram
آن را می گیرم.

Excuse me, where do I pay?	bebaxšid, sandoq kojāst?
	ببخشید، صندوق کجاست؟
Will you pay in cash or credit card?	be surat-e naqdi ya bā kārt-e e'tebāri pardāxt mikonid?
	به صورت نقدی یا با کارت اعتباری پرداخت می کنید؟
In cash | with credit card	naqdi | bā kārt-e e'tebāri
	با کارت اعتباری ا نقدی

Do you want the receipt?	resid mixāhid?
	رسید می خواهید؟
Yes, please.	bale, lotfan
	بله، لطفاً.
No, it's OK.	xeyr, niyāzi nist
	خیر، نیازی نیست.
Thank you. Have a nice day!	mamnum ruzetān xoš!
	ممنون، روزتان خوش!

In town

Excuse me, please.	bebaxšid, … ...،ببخشید
I'm looking for …	donbāl-e … migardam دنبال...می گردم
the subway	metro مترو
my hotel	hotel-e man هتل من
the movie theater	cinamā سینما
a taxi stand	istgāh-e tāksi ایستگاه تاکسی
an ATM	xodpardāz خودپرداز
a foreign exchange office	daftar-e sarāfi دفتر صرافی
an internet café	kāfinet کافی نت
… street	xiyābān-e … ...خیابان
this place	in makān این مکان
Do you know where … is?	āyā midānid … kojāst آیامی دانید...کجاست؟
Which street is this?	in če xiyābāni ast? این چه خیابانی است؟
Show me where we are right now.	lotfan be man nešān bedahid alān kojā hastim لطفأ به من نشان بدهید الان کجا هستیم.
Can I get there on foot?	mitavānam piyāde beravam? می توانم پیاده بروم؟
Do you have a map of the city?	naqše-ye šahr rā dārid? نقشه شهر را دارید؟
How much is a ticket to get in?	qeymat-e yek bilit čand ast? قیمت یک بلیط چند است؟
Can I take pictures here?	āyā mitavānam aks begiram? آیا می توانم عکس بگیرم؟
Are you open?	bāz hastid? باز هستید؟

When do you open?

če sāati bāz mikonid?

چه ساعتی باز می کنید؟

When do you close?

če sāati mibandid?

چه ساعتی می بندید؟

Money

money	pul
	پول
cash	pul-e naqd
	پول نقد
paper money	eskenās
	اسکناس
loose change	pul-e xord
	پول خرد
check | change | tip	surat hesāb | pul-e xord | an'ām
	انعام ا پول خرد ا صورت حساب

credit card	kārt-e e'tebāri
	کارت اعتباری
wallet	kif-e pul
	کیف پول
to buy	xaridan
	خریدن
to pay	pardāxt kardan
	پرداخت کردن
fine	jarime
	جریمه
free	rāygān
	رایگان

Where can I buy ...?	kojā mitavānam ... bexaram?
	کجا می توانم...بخرم؟
Is the bank open now?	āyā alān bānk bāz ast?
	آیا الان بانک باز است؟
When does it open?	če sāati bāz mikonad?
	چه ساعتی بازمی کند؟
When does it close?	če sāati mibandad?
	چه ساعتی می بندد؟

How much?	čand ast?
	چنداست؟
How much is this?	qeymat-e ān čand ast?
	قیمت آن چند است؟
That's too expensive.	xeyli gerān ast
	خیلی گران است.

Excuse me, where do I pay?	bebaxšid, sandoq kojāst?
	ببخشید،صندوق کجاست؟
Check, please.	surat hesāb, lotfan
	صورت حساب، لطفاً.

Can I pay by credit card?   mitavānam bā kārt bepardāzam?
می توانم با کارت بپردازم؟

Is there an ATM here?   āyā injā xodpardāz hast?
آیا اینجا خودپرداز هست؟

I'm looking for an ATM.   donbāl-e yek xodpardāz migardam
دنبال یک خودپرداز می گردم.

I'm looking for a foreign exchange office.   donbāl-e sarrāfi migardam
دنبال صرافی می گردم.

I'd like to change …   mixāham … avaz konam
می خواهم...عوض کنم.

What is the exchange rate?   nerx-e arz čeqadr ast?
نرخ ارز چقدر است؟

Do you need my passport?   āyā gozarnāme-ye man rā lāzem dārid?
آیا گذرنامه من را لازم دارید؟

Time

What time is it?	sāat čand ast? ساعت چند است؟
When?	key? کی؟
At what time?	če sāati? چه ساعتی؟
now | later | after ...	alān | dirtar | ba'd بعد | دیرتر | الان
one o'clock	sāat-e yek ساعت یک
one fifteen	sāat-e yek-o-rob ساعت یک و ربع
one thirty	sāat-e yek-o-nim ساعت یک و نیم
one forty-five	yek rob be do یک ربع به دو
one | two | three	yek | do | se سه | دو | یک
four | five | six	čāhār | panj | šeš شش | پنج | چهار
seven | eight | nine	haft | hašt | noh نه | هشت | هفت
ten | eleven | twelve	dah | yāzdah | davāzdah دوازده | یازده | ده
in ...	tā ... digar تا...دیگر
five minutes	panj daqiqe پنج دقیقه
ten minutes	dah daqiqe ده دقیقه
fifteen minutes	pānzdah daqiqe پانزده دقیقه
twenty minutes	bist daqiqe بیست دقیقه
half an hour	nim sāat نیم ساعت
an hour	yek sāat یک ساعت

in the morning	sobh صبح
early in the morning	sobh-e zud صبح زود
this morning	emruz sobh امروزصبح
tomorrow morning	fardā sobh فردا صبح
in the middle of the day	zohr ظهر
in the afternoon	ba'd az zohr بعد ازظهر
in the evening	šab شب
tonight	emšab امشب
at night	šab شب
yesterday	diruz دیروز
today	emruz امروز
tomorrow	fardā فردا
the day after tomorrow	pas fardā پس فردا
What day is it today?	emruz če ruzi ast? امروزچه روزی است؟
It's ...	emruz ... ast امروز...است
Monday	došanbe دوشنبه
Tuesday	sešanbe سه شنبه
Wednesday	čāhāršanbe چهارشنبه
Thursday	panjšanbe پنجشنبه
Friday	jom'e جمعه
Saturday	šanbe شنبه
Sunday	yekšanbe یکشنبه

Greetings. Introductions

Hello.
salām
سلام.

Pleased to meet you.
xošbaxtam
خوشبختم.

Me too.
man ham hamintor
من هم همینطور.

I'd like you to meet …
… rā be šomā mo'arefi mikonam
...را به شما معرفی می کنم

Nice to meet you.
az didāretan xošbaxtam
از دیدارتان خوشبختم.

How are you?
hāletān četor ast?
حالتان چطور است؟

My name is …
esm-e man … ast
اسم من...است.

His name is …
esm-e u … ast
اسم او...است.

Her name is …
esm-e u … ast
اسم او...است.

What's your name?
esm-e šomā čist?
اسم شما چیست؟

What's his name?
esm-e u čist?
اسم او چیست؟

What's her name?
esm-e u čist?
اسم او چیست؟

What's your last name?
nām xānevādegi-ye šomā čist?
نام خانوادگی شما چیست؟

You can call me …
mitavānid man rā … sedā konid
می توانید من را...صدا کنید

Where are you from?
ahl-e kojāhastid?
اهل کجا هستید؟

I'm from …
ahl-e … hastam
اهل...هستم.

What do you do for a living?
šoql-e šomā čist?
شغل شما چیست؟

Who is this?
kiye?
کیه؟

Who is he?
u kist?
اوکیست؟

Who is she?
u kist?
اوکیست؟

Who are they?
ānhā ki hatand?
آنها کی هستند؟

This is …	u … ast
	تو...اسـت
my friend (masc.)	dust-e man
	دوسـت من
my friend (fem.)	dust-e man
	دوسـت من
my husband	šohar-e mn
	شوهر من
my wife	zan-e man
	زن من

my father	pedar-e man
	پدر من
my mother	mādar-e man
	مادر من
my brother	barādar-e man
	برادر من
my sister	xāhar-e man
	خواهر من
my son	pesar-e man
	پسر من
my daughter	doxtar-e man
	دختر من

This is our son.	pesar-e māst
	پسر ماسـت.
This is our daughter.	doxtar-e māst
	دخترماسـت.
These are my children.	farzandān-e man hastand
	فرزندان من هسـتند.
These are our children.	farzandān-e mā hastand
	فرزندان ما هسـتند.

Farewells

Good bye!	xodāhāfez! خداحافظ!
Bye! (inform.)	bāy bāy! بای بای!
See you tomorrow.	tā fardā تا فردا.
See you soon.	tā be zudi تا به زودی.
See you at seven.	tā sāat-e haft تا ساعت هفت.
Have fun!	xoš begzarad! خوش بگذرد!
Talk to you later.	hamdigar rā ba'dan mibinim همدیگررا بعدا می بینیم.
Have a nice weekend.	āxar-e hafte xoš آخر هفته خوش.
Good night.	šab xoš شب خوش.
It's time for me to go.	vaqt-e raftan-e man ast وقت رفتن من است.
I have to go.	bāyad beravam باید بروم.
I will be right back.	zud barmigardam زود بر می گردم.
It's late.	dir ast دیراست.
I have to get up early.	bāyad zud az xāb bidār šavam باید زود از خواب بیدار شوم.
I'm leaving tomorrow.	fardā be safar miravam فردا به سفر می روم.
We're leaving tomorrow.	fardā be safar miravim فردا به سفر می رویم.
Have a nice trip!	safar be xeyr! سفر به خیر!
It was nice meeting you.	az āšnāyi bā šomā xošbaxtam ازآشنایی با شما خوشبختم.
It was nice talking to you.	az sohbat bā šomā xošhāl šodam ازصحبت با شما خوشحال شدم.
Thanks for everything.	barāye hame čiz mamnun برای همه چیز ممنونم.

I had a very good time.	oqāt-e xubi rā gozarāndam
	اوقات خوبی را گذراندم.
We had a very good time.	oqāt-e xubi rā gozarāndim
	اوقات خوبی را گذراندیم.
It was really great.	xeyli xoš gozašt
	خیلی خوش گذشت.
I'm going to miss you.	delam barāyetān tang mišavad
	دلم برایتان تنگ می شود.
We're going to miss you.	delamān barāyetān tang mišavad
	دلمان برایتان تنگ می شود.
Good luck!	movaffaq bāšid!
	موفق باشید!
Say hi to …	salām-e an rā be … beresānid
	سلام من را به...برسانید.

Foreign language

I don't understand.	motevajjeh nemišavam متوجه نمی شوم.
Write it down, please.	lotfan ānrā benevisid لطفاً آنرا بنویسید.
Do you speak ...?	āyā ... sohbat mikonid آیا...صحبت می کنید؟

I speak a little bit of ...	kami ... sohbat mikonam کمی...صحبت می کنم
English	ingilisi انگلیسی
Turkish	torki ترکی
Arabic	arabi عربی
French	farānsavi فرانسوی

German	ālmāni آلمانی
Italian	itāliyāyi ایتالیایی
Spanish	espāniyāyi اسپانیایی
Portuguese	porteqāli پرتغالی
Chinese	čini چینی
Japanese	žāponi ژاپنی

Can you repeat that, please.	lotfan mitavānid tekrār konid لطفاً می توانید تکرار کنید.
I understand.	motevajjeh mišavam متوجه می شوم.
I don't understand.	motevajjeh nemišavam متوجه نمی شوم.
Please speak more slowly.	lotfan aheste tar sohbat konid لطفاً آهسته ترصحبت کنید.

| Is that correct? (Am I saying it right?) | āyā dorost miguyam?
آیا درست می گویم؟ |
| What is this? (What does this mean?) | ya'ni če?
یعنی چه؟ |

Apologies

Excuse me, please.	bebaxsid, lotfan
	ببخشید، لطفاً.
I'm sorry.	moteasefam
	متأسفم.
I'm really sorry.	vage'an moteasefam
	واقعا متأسفم.
Sorry, it's my fault.	moteasefam, taqsir-e man ast
	متأسفم، تقصیرمن است.
My mistake.	man eštebāh kardam
	من اشتباه کردم.
May I ...?	mitavānam ...?
	می توانم...؟
Do you mind if I ...?	barāye šomā eškāli nadārad agar man ...?
	برای شما اشکالی ندارد اگرمن...؟
It's OK.	mohem nist
	مهم نیست.
It's all right.	moškeli nist
	مشکلی نیست.
Don't worry about it.	mas'alei nist
	مسئله ای نیست.

Agreement

Yes.	bale بله
Yes, sure.	bale, albate بله، البته.
OK (Good!)	xub. خوب.
Very well.	xeyli xub خیلی خوب.
Certainly!	albate! البته!
I agree.	movāfeq hastam موافق هستم.
That's correct.	dorost ast درست است.
That's right.	dorost ast درست است.
You're right.	rāst miguyid راست می گویید.
I don't mind.	moxālef nistam مخالف نیستم.
Absolutely right.	kāmelan dorost ast کاملا درست است.
It's possible.	momken ast ممکن است.
That's a good idea.	fekr-e xubi ast فکر خوبی است.
I can't say no.	nemitavānam na beguyam نمی توانم نه بگویم.
I'd be happy to.	xošhāl xāham šod خوشحال خواهم شد.
With pleasure.	bā kamāl-e meyl با کمال میل.

Refusal. Expressing doubt

No.	xeyr
	خیر
Certainly not.	aslan
	اصلا.
I don't agree.	movāfeq nistam
	موافق نیستم.
I don't think so.	fekr nemikonam
	فکر نمی کنم.
It's not true.	dorost nist
	درست نیست.

You are wrong.	eštebāh mikonid
	اشتباه می کنید.
I think you are wrong.	fekr mikonam ke eštebāh mikonid
	فکر می کنم که اشتباه می کنید.

I'm not sure.	motma'en nistam
	مطمئن نیستم
It's impossible.	qeyre momken ast
	غیر ممکن است.
Nothing of the kind (sort)!	be hič onvān!
	به هیچ عنوان!

The exact opposite.	bar aks!
	برعکس!
I'm against it.	moxālefam
	مخالفم.

I don't care.	barāyam farqi nemikonad
	برایم فرقی نمی کند.
I have no idea.	hič nazari nadāram
	هیچ نظری ندارم.
I doubt it.	šak dāram
	شک دارم.

Sorry, I can't.	moteasefam, nemitavānam
	متاسفم، نمی توانم.
Sorry, I don't want to.	moteasefam, nemixāham
	متاسفم، نمی خواهم.

Thank you, but I don't need this.	mamnun vali barāyam jāleb nist
	ممنون ولی برایم جالب نیست.
It's getting late.	dir šode ast
	دیر شده است.

I have to get up early.

bāyad zud az xāb bidār šavam

باید زود از خواب بیدار شوم.

I don't feel well.

hālam xub nist

حالم خوب نیست.

Expressing gratitude

Thank you.	mamnun
	ممنون.
Thank you very much.	xeyli mamnun
	خیلی ممنون.
I really appreciate it.	besyār sepāsgozāram
	بسیار سپاسگزارم.
I'm really grateful to you.	vaqean az šomā motešakkeram
	واقعا از شما متشکرم.
We are really grateful to you.	vaqean az šomā motešakkerim
	واقعا از شما متشکریم.
Thank you for your time.	mamnun ke vaqt gozāštid
	ممنون که وقت گذاشتید.
Thanks for everything.	barāye hame čiz mamnun
	برای همه چیز ممنونم.
Thank you for ...	mamnun barāye ...
	ممنون برای...
your help	komak-e šomā
	کمک شما
a nice time	lahezāt-e xubi ke gozarāndim
	لحظات خوبی که گذراندیم
a wonderful meal	qazā-ye laziz
	غذای لذیذ
a pleasant evening	in šab-e āli
	این شب عالی
a wonderful day	in ruz-e foqol'āde
	این روز فوق العاده
an amazing journey	in safar-e xareqol'āde
	این سفر خارق العاده
Don't mention it.	xāheš mikonam
	خواهش می کنم.
You are welcome.	xāheš mikonam
	خواهش می کنم.
Any time.	bā kamāl-e meyl
	با کمال میل.
My pleasure.	bāes-e xošhāli bud
	باعث خوشحالی بود.
Forget it.	qābeli nadāšt
	قابلی نداشت.
Don't worry about it.	mas'alei nist
	مسئله ای نیست.

Congratulations. Best wishes

Congratulations!	mobārak bāšad! !مبارک باشد
Happy birthday!	tavalodet mobārak! !تولدت مبارک
Merry Christmas!	krismas mobārak! !کریسمس مبارک
Happy New Year!	sāl-e no mobārak! !سال نو مبارک
Happy Easter!	eyd-e pāk mobārak! !عید پاک مبارک
Happy Hanukkah!	hānokā mobārak! !هانوکا مبارک
I'd like to propose a toast.	be salāmati benušim .به سلامتی بنوشیم
Cheers!	be salāmati! !به سلامتی
Let's drink to …!	be salāmati-ye…benušim! !بنوشیم...به سلامتی
To our success!	be salāmati-ye movaffaqiyat-e mā! !به سلامتی موفقیت ما
To your success!	be salāmati-ye movaffaqiyat-e šomā! !به سلامتی موفقیت شما
Good luck!	movaffaq bāšid! !موفق باشید
Have a nice day!	ruz xoš! !روز خوش
Have a good holiday!	tatilāt xoš! ! تعطیلات خوش
Have a safe journey!	safar be xeyr! !سفر به خیر
I hope you get better soon!	be ārezuye salāmati-ye zudtar-e šomā. .به آرزوی سلامتی زودتر شما

Socializing

Why are you sad?	čerā nārāhat hastid? چرا ناراحت هستید؟
Smile! Cheer up!	labxand bezanid! البخند بزنید!
Are you free tonight?	emšab āzād hastid? امشب آزاد هستید؟
May I offer you a drink?	mitavānam be yek nušidani da'vatetān konam? می توانم به یک نوشیدنی دعوتتان کنم؟
Would you like to dance?	āyā mixāhid beraqsid? آیا می خواهید برقصید؟
Let's go to the movies.	āyā dust dārid be cinamā beravim? آیا دوست داریدبه سینما برویم؟
May I invite you to ...?	mitavānam šomā rā ... da'vat konam می توانم شما را ...دعوت کنم
a restaurant	be resturān به رستوران
the movies	be cinamā به سینما
the theater	be teātr به تئاتر
go for a walk	be gardeš به گردش
At what time?	če sāati? چه ساعتی؟
tonight	emšab امشب
at six	sāat-e šeš ساعت شش
at seven	sāat-e haft ساعت هفت
at eight	sāat-e hašt ساعت هشت
at nine	sāat-e noh ساعت نه
Do you like it here?	āyā in mahal rā dust dārid? آیا این محل را دوست دارید؟
Are you here with someone?	āyā bā kasi be injā āmadeid? آیا با کسی اینجا آمده اید؟

I'm with my friend.	bā dustam hastam
	با دوستم هستم.
I'm with my friends.	bā dustānam hastam
	با دوستانم هستم.
No, I'm alone.	na,tanhā hastam
	نه، تنها هستم.

Do you have a boyfriend?	dust pesar dāri?
	دوست پسرداری؟
I have a boyfriend.	dust pesar dāram
	دوست پسردارم.
Do you have a girlfriend?	dust doxtar dāri?
	دوست دختر داری؟
I have a girlfriend.	dust doxtar dāram
	دوست دختر دارم.

Can I see you again?	mitavānam dobāre bebinametān?
	می توانم دوباره ببینمتان؟
Can I call you?	mitavānam behetān telefon bezanam?
	می توانم بهتان تلفن بزنم؟
Call me. (Give me a call.)	behem telefn bezan
	بهم تلفن بزن.
What's your number?	šomāre-ye telefonet čist?
	شماره تلفنت چیست؟
I miss you.	delam barāyat tang šode ast
	دلم برایت تنگ شده است.

You have a beautiful name.	esm-e gašangi dārid
	اسم قشنگی دارید.
I love you.	dustat dāram
	دوستت دارم.
Will you marry me?	mixāhi bā man ezdevāj koni?
	می خواهی با من ازدواج کنی؟
You're kidding!	šuxi mikonid!
	شوخی می کنید!
I'm just kidding.	šuxi mikonam
	شوخی می کنم.

Are you serious?	jeddi miguyid?
	جدی می گویید؟
I'm serious.	jeddi miguyam
	جدی می گویم.
Really?!	vāqean?!
	واقعا؟!
It's unbelievable!	bāvar nakadani ast
	باورنکردنی است
I don't believe you.	harfetān rā bāvar nemikonam
	حرفتان را باور نمی کنم.
I can't.	nemitavānam
	نمی توانم.
I don't know.	nemidānam
	نمی دانم.

I don't understand you.

harfetān rā nemifahmam

حرفتان را نمی فهمم.

Please go away.

lotfan beravid!

!لطفاً بروید

Leave me alone!

lotfan marā rāhat begozārid!

!مرا راحت بگذارید

I can't stand him.

nemitavānam u rā tahamol konam

نمی توانم او را تحمل کنم.

You are disgusting!

šomā monzajer konande hastid!

!شما منزجر کننده هستید

I'll call the police!

polis rā sedā mizanam!

!پلیس را صدا می زنم

Sharing impressions. Emotions

I like it.	in rā dust dāram این را دوست دارم.
Very nice.	xeyli xub ast خیلی خوب است.
That's great!	āli ast! عالی است!
It's not bad.	bad nist بد نیست.
I don't like it.	in rā dust nadāram این را دوست ندارم.
It's not good.	xub nist خوب نیست.
It's bad.	bad ast بد است.
It's very bad.	aslan xub nist اصلا خوب نیست.
It's disgusting.	mozajer knande ast منزجر کننده است.
I'm happy.	xošhāl hastam خوشحال هستم.
I'm content.	xošbaxt hastam خوشبخت هستم.
I'm in love.	āšeq hastam عاشق هستم.
I'm calm.	ārām hastam آرام هستم.
I'm bored.	kesel hastam کسل هستم.
I'm tired.	xaste-am خسته ام.
I'm sad.	nārāhat hastam ناراحت هستم.
I'm frightened.	mitarsam می ترسم.
I'm angry.	asabāni hastam عصبانی هستم.
I'm worried.	negarān hastam نگران هستم.
I'm nervous.	asabi hastam عصبی هستم.

I'm jealous. (envious)

hasud hastam

حسود هستم.

I'm surprised.

mote'ajeb hastam

متعجب هستم.

I'm perplexed.

bohtzade hastam

بهت زده هستم.

Problems. Accidents

I've got a problem.	yek moškel dāram یک مشکل دارم.
We've got a problem.	yek moškel dārim یک مشکل داریم.
I'm lost.	gom šodeam گم شده ام.
I missed the last bus (train).	āxarin otobus (qatār) rā az dast dādeam آخرین اتوبوس (قطار) را از دست دادم.
I don't have any money left.	digar pul nadāram دیگر پول ندارم.

I've lost my ...	...-am rā gom kardeam ...ام راگم کرده ام.
Someone stole my ...	...-am rā dozdidand ...ام را دزدیدند.

passport	gozarnāme گذرنامه
wallet	kif-e pul کیف پول
papers	madārek مدارک
ticket	bilit بلیط

money	pul پول
handbag	kif-e dasti کیف دستی
camera	durbin-e akkāsi دوربین عکاسی
laptop	laptāp لپ تاپ
tablet computer	tablet تبلت
mobile phone	mobāyl موبایل

Help me!	komak! !کمک
What's happened?	če ettefāqi oftāde ast? چه اتفاقی افتاده است؟
fire	ātaš suzi آتش سوزی

shooting	tirandāzi
	تیراندازی
murder	qatl
	قتل
explosion	enfejār
	انفجار
fight	da'vā
	دعوا

Call the police!	polis rā xabar konid!
	!پلیس را خبر کنید
Please hurry up!	lotfan ajale konid!
	!لطفاً عجله کنید
I'm looking for the police station.	donbāl-e edāre-ye polis migardam
	.دنبال اداره پلیس می گردم
I need to make a call.	niyāz dāram telefon bezanam
	.نیازدارم تلفن بزنم
May I use your phone?	mitavānam az telefon-e šomā estefāde konam?
	می توانم از تلفن شما استفاده کنم؟

I've been …	man mored-e … qarār gereftam
	من مورد...قرار گرفتم
mugged	man mored-e hamle qarār gereftam
	من مورد حمله قرار گرفتم
robbed	man mored-e dozdi qarār gereftam
	من مورد دزدی قرار گرفتم
raped	man mored-e tajāvoz qarār gereftam
	من مورد تجاوز قرار گرفتم
attacked (beaten up)	man kotak xordam
	من کتک خوردم

Are you all right?	xub hastid?
	خوب هستید؟
Did you see who it was?	didid ki bud?
	دیدید کی بود؟
Would you be able to recognize the person?	āyā mitavānid in šaxs ra šenāsāyi konid?
	آیامی توانید این شخص را شناسایی کنید؟
Are you sure?	motma'en hastid?
	مطمئن هستید؟

Please calm down.	lotfan ārām bašid
	.لطفاً آرام باشید
Take it easy!	ārām bāšid!
	!آرام باشید
Don't worry!	mas'alei nist
	.مسئله ای نیست
Everything will be fine.	hame čiz be xubi xāhad gozašt
	.همه چیز به خوبی خواهد گذشت
Everything's all right.	hame čiz xub ast
	.همه چیز خوب است

Come here, please.

lotfan biyāyid injā

لطفاً بیایید اینجا.

I have some questions for you.

az šomā cand soāl dāram

از شما چند سوال دارم.

Wait a moment, please.

lotfan yek lahze montazer bemānid

لطفاً یک لحظه منتظر بمانید.

Do you have any I.D.?

kārt-e šenāsāyi dārid?

کارت شناسایی دارید؟

Thanks. You can leave now.

mamnun, mitavānid beravid

ممنون. می توانید بروید.

Hands behind your head!

dast-hā rā pošt-e sar begozārid!

دست ها را پشت سر بگذارید!

You're under arrest!

šomā bāzdāšt hastid!

شما بازداشت هستید!

Health problems

Please help me.	lotfan be man komak konid
	لطفاً به من کمک کنید.
I don't feel well.	hālam xub nist
	حالم خوب نیست.
My husband doesn't feel well.	hāl-e šoharam xub nist
	حال شوهرم خوب نیست.
My son ...	pesaram
	پسرم...
My father ...	pedaram
	پدرم...
My wife doesn't feel well.	hāl-e zanam xub nist
	حال زنم خوب نیست.
My daughter ...	doxtaram
	دخترم...
My mother ...	mādaram
	مادرم...
I've got a ...	... dard dāram
	...درد دارم
headache	sar
	سر
sore throat	galu
	گلو
stomach ache	me'de
	معده
toothache	dandān
	دندان
I feel dizzy.	sargije dāram
	سرگیجه دارم.
He has a fever.	tab dāram
	تب دارم.
She has a fever.	u tab dārad
	او تب دارد.
I can't breathe.	nemitavānam nafas bekešam
	نمی توانم نفس بکشم.
I'm short of breath.	nafaskešidan barāyam saxt ast
	نفس کشیدن برایم سخت است.
I am asthmatic.	āsm dāram
	آسم دارم.
I am diabetic.	diyābet dāram
	دیابت دارم.

I can't sleep.

nemitavānam bexābam

نمی توانم بخوابم.

food poisoning

masmumiyat-e qazāyi

مسمومیت غذایی

It hurts here.

injāyam dard mikonad

اینجایم درد میکند.

Help me!

komak!

!کمک

I am here!

injā hastam!

!اینجا هستم

We are here!

injā hastim!

!اینجا هستیم

Get me out of here!

man rā az inja xārej konid!

!من را از اینجا خارج کنید

I need a doctor.

ehtiyāj be doktor daram

احتیاج به دکتر دارم.

I can't move.

nimitavānam tekān boxoram

نمی توانم تکان بخورم.

I can't move my legs.

nemitavānam pāhāyam ra tekān bedaham

نمی توانم پاهایم را تکان بدهم.

I have a wound.

zaxmi šodeam

زخمی شده ام.

Is it serious?

jeddi ast?

جدی است؟

My documents are in my pocket.

madārekam dar jibam hastand

مدارکم در جیبم هستند.

Calm down!

ārām bāšid!

!آرام باشید

May I use your phone?

mitavānam az telefon-e šomā estefāde konam?

می توانم از تلفن شما استفاده کنم؟

Call an ambulance!

āmbulāns xabar konid!

!آمبولانس خبر کنید

It's urgent!

fori ast!

!فوری است

It's an emergency!

uržansi ast!

!اورژانسی است

Please hurry up!

lotfan ajale konid!

!لطفاً عجله کنید

Would you please call a doctor?

lotfan doktor xabar konid

لطفاً دکتر خبر کنید.

Where is the hospital?

bimārestān kojast

بیمارستان کجاست؟

How are you feeling?

hāletān četor ast?

حالتان چطور است؟

Are you all right?

hame čiz xub ast?
همه چیز خوب است؟

What's happened?

če ettefāqi oftāde ast?
چه اتفاقی افتاده است؟

I feel better now.

alān hālam behtar ast
الان حالم بهتر است.

It's OK.

hame čiz xub ast
همه چیز خوب است.

It's all right.

xub hastam
خوب هستم.

At the pharmacy

pharmacy (drugstore)	dāruxāne داروخانه
24-hour pharmacy	dāruxāne-ye šabāne ruzi داروخانه شبانه روزی
Where is the closest pharmacy?	nazdiktarin dāruxāne kojāst? نزدیک ترین داروخانه کجاست؟

Is it open now?	alān bāz ast? الان باز است؟
At what time does it open?	če sāati bāz mikonad? چه ساعتی باز می کند؟
At what time does it close?	če sāati mibandad? چه ساعتی می بندد؟

Is it far?	dur ast? دور است؟
Can I get there on foot?	mitavānam piyāde beravam? می توانم پیاده بروم؟
Can you show me on the map?	mitavānid ruye naqše nešānam bedahid? می توانید روی نقشه نشانم بدهید؟

Please give me something for ...	mitavānid daruyi barāye ... be man bedahid می توانید دارویی برای...به من بدهید
a headache	sar dard سر درد
a cough	sorfe سرفه
a cold	sarmā xordegi سرماخوردگی
the flu	grip گریپ

a fever	tab تب
a stomach ache	me'de dard معده درد
nausea	tahavvo' تهوع
diarrhea	eshāl اسهال
constipation	yobusat یبوست

pain in the back	pošt dard
	پشت درد
chest pain	sine dard
	سینه درد
side stitch	pahlu dard
	پهلو درد
abdominal pain	šekam dard
	شکم درد
pill	qors
	قرص
ointment, cream	pomād, kerem
	پماد کرم
syrup	šarbat
	شربت
spray	esperey
	اسپری
drops	qatre
	قطره
You need to go to the hospital.	bāyad be bimarestān beravid
	بایدبه بیمارستان بروید.
health insurance	bime-ye darmān
	بیمه درمان
prescription	nosxe
	نسخه
insect repellant	made-ye daf'e hašarāt
	ماده دفع حشرات
Band Aid	bāndaž-e časbdār
	باانداژ چسبدار

The bare minimum

Excuse me, ...	bebaxšid, ... ببخشید،....
Hello.	salām سلام.
Thank you.	mamnun ممنون
Good bye.	xodāhāfez خداحافظ.
Yes.	bale بله
No.	xeyr خیر
I don't know.	nemidānam نمی دانم.
Where? | Where to? | When?	kojā? | kojā? | key? کی؟ | کجا؟ | کجا؟

I need ...	be ... ehtiyāj dāram به...أحتیاج دارم
I want ...	mixāham ... ...می خواهم
Do you have ...?	āyā ... dārid? آیا...دارید؟
Is there a ... here?	āyā injā ... hast? آیا اینجا ...هست؟
May I ...?	mitavānam ...? می توانم...؟
..., please (polite request)	lotfan لطفاً

I'm looking for ...	donbāl-e ... migardam دنبال...می گردم.
restroom	tuālet توالت
ATM	xodpardāz خودپرداز
pharmacy (drugstore)	dāruxāne داروخانه
hospital	bimārestān بیمارستان
police station	edāre-ye polis اداره پلیس
subway	istgāh-e metro ایستگاه مترو

taxi	tāksi تاکسی
train station	istgāh-e qatār ایستگاه قطار

My name is …	esm-e man … ast اسم من...است.
What's your name?	esm-e šomā čist? اسم شما چیست؟
Could you please help me?	lotfan mitavānid komakam konid? لطفاً می توانید کمکم کنید؟
I've got a problem.	yek moškel dāram یک مشکل دارم.
I don't feel well.	hālam xub nist حالم خوب نیست.
Call an ambulance!	āmbulāns xabar konid! آمبولانس خبر کنید!
May I make a call?	mitavānam yek telefon bezanam? می توانم یک تلفن بزنم؟

I'm sorry.	ma'zerat mixāham معذرت می خواهم.
You're welcome.	xāheš mikonam خواهش می کنم.

I, me	man من
you (inform.)	to تو
he	u او
she	u او
they (masc.)	an-hā آنها
they (fem.)	an-hā آنها
we	mā ما
you (pl)	šomā شما
you (sg, form.)	šomā شما

ENTRANCE	vorudi ورودی
EXIT	xoruji خروجی
OUT OF ORDER	xarāb خراب
CLOSED	baste بسته

OPEN   bāz

باز

FOR WOMEN   zanāne

زنانه

FOR MEN   mardāne

مردانه

CONCISE DICTIONARY

This section contains more than 1,500 useful words arranged alphabetically. The dictionary includes a lot of gastronomic terms and will be helpful when ordering food at a restaurant or buying groceries

T&P Books Publishing

DICTIONARY CONTENTS

T&P Books Publishing

time	zamān	زمان
hour	sā'at	ساعت
half an hour	nim sā'at	نیم ساعت
minute	daqiqe	دقیقه
second	sānie	ثانیه
today (adv)	emruz	امروز
tomorrow (adv)	fardā	فردا
yesterday (adv)	diruz	دیروز
Monday	došanbe	دوشنبه
Tuesday	se šanbe	سه شنبه
Wednesday	čāhāršanbe	چهارشنبه
Thursday	panj šanbe	پنج شنبه
Friday	jom'e	جمعه
Saturday	šanbe	شنبه
Sunday	yek šanbe	یک شنبه
day	ruz	روز
working day	ruz-e kāri	روز کاری
public holiday	ruz-e jašn	روز جشن
weekend	āxar-e hafte	آخر هفته
week	hafte	هفته
last week (adv)	hafte-ye gozašte	هفته گذشته
next week (adv)	hafte-ye āyande	هفته آینده
sunrise	tolu-'e āftāb	طلوع آفتاب
sunset	qorub	غروب
in the morning	sobh	صبح
in the afternoon	ba'd az zohr	بعد ازظهر
in the evening	asr	عصر
tonight (this evening)	emšab	امشب
at night	šab	شب
midnight	nesfe šab	نصفه شب
January	žānvie	ژانویه
February	fevriye	فوریه
March	mārs	مارس
April	āvril	آوریل
May	meh	مه
June	žuan	ژوئن

July	žuiye	ژوئیه
August	owt	اوت
September	septāmbr	سپتامبر
October	oktobr	اکتبر
November	novāmbr	نوامبر
December	desāmr	دسامبر

in spring	dar bahār	در بهار
in summer	dar tābestān	در تابستان
in fall	dar pāyiz	در پاییز
in winter	dar zemestān	در زمستان

month	māh	ماه
season (summer, etc.)	fasl	فصل
year	sāl	سال
century	qarn	قرن

2. Numbers. Numerals

digit, figure	raqam	رقم
number	adad	عدد
minus sign	manfi	منفی
plus sign	mosbat	مثبت
sum, total	jam'-e kol	جمع کل

first (adj)	avvalin	اولین
second (adj)	dovvomin	دومین
third (adj)	sevvomin	سومین

0 zero	sefr	صفر
1 one	yek	یک
2 two	do	دو
3 three	se	سه
4 four	čāhār	چهار

5 five	panj	پنج
6 six	šeš	شش
7 seven	haft	هفت
8 eight	hašt	هشت
9 nine	neh	نه
10 ten	dah	ده

11 eleven	yāzdah	یازده
12 twelve	davāzdah	دوازده
13 thirteen	sizdah	سیزده
14 fourteen	čāhārdah	چهارده
15 fifteen	pānzdah	پانزده

| 16 sixteen | šānzdah | شانزده |
| 17 seventeen | hefdah | هفده |

| 18 eighteen | hijdah | هیجده |
| 19 nineteen | nuzdah | نوزده |

20 twenty	bist	بیست
30 thirty	si	سی
40 forty	čehel	چهل
50 fifty	panjāh	پنجاه

60 sixty	šast	شصت
70 seventy	haftād	هفتاد
80 eighty	haštād	هشتاد
90 ninety	navad	نود

100 one hundred	sad	صد
200 two hundred	devist	دویست
300 three hundred	sisad	سیصد
400 four hundred	čāhārsad	چهارصد
500 five hundred	pānsad	پانصد

600 six hundred	šeššad	ششصد
700 seven hundred	haftsad	هفتصد
800 eight hundred	haštsad	هشتصد
900 nine hundred	nohsad	نهصد
1000 one thousand	hezār	هزار

| 10000 ten thousand | dah hezār | ده هزار |
| one hundred thousand | sad hezār | صد هزار |

| million | milyun | میلیون |
| billion | milyārd | میلیارد |

3. Humans. Family

man (adult male)	mard	مرد
young man	mard-e javān	مرد جوان
teenager	nowjavān	نوجوان
woman	zan	زن
girl (young woman)	doxtar	دختر

age	sen	سن
adult (adj)	bāleq	بالغ
middle-aged (adj)	miyānsāl	میانسال
elderly (adj)	sālmand	سالمند
old (adj)	mosen	مسن

old man	pirmard	پیرمرد
old woman	pirzan	پیرزن
retirement	mostamerri	مستمری
to retire (from job)	bāznešaste šodan	بازنشسته شدن
retiree	bāznešaste	بازنشسته

mother	mādar	مادر
father	pedar	پدر
son	pesar	پسر
daughter	doxtar	دختر
brother	barādar	برادر
elder brother	barādar-e bozorg	برادر بزرگ
younger brother	barādar-e kučak	برادر کوچک
sister	xāhar	خواهر
elder sister	xāhar-e bozorg	خواهر بزرگ
younger sister	xāhar-e kučak	خواهر کوچک
parents	vāledeyn	والدین
child	kudak	کودک
children	bače-hā	بچه ها
stepmother	nāmādari	نامادری
stepfather	nāpedari	ناپدری
grandmother	mādarbozorg	مادربزرگ
grandfather	pedar-bozorg	پدربزرگ
grandson	nave	نوه
granddaughter	nave	نوه
grandchildren	nave-hā	نوه ها
uncle	amu	عمو
aunt	xāle yā amme	خاله یا عمه
nephew	barādar-zāde	برادرزاده
niece	xāhar-zāde	خواهرزاده
wife	zan	زن
husband	šowhar	شوهر
married (masc.)	mote'ahhel	متاهل
married (fem.)	mote'ahhel	متاهل
widow	bive zan	بیوه زن
widower	bive	بیوه
name (first name)	esm	اسم
surname (last name)	nām-e xānevādegi	نام خانوادگی
relative	xišāvand	خویشاوند
friend (masc.)	dust	دوست
friendship	dusti	دوستی
partner	šarik	شریک
superior (n)	ra'is	رئیس
colleague	hamkār	همکار
neighbors	hamsāye-hā	همسایه ها

4. Human body

| organism (body) | orgānism | ارگانیسم |
| body | badan | بدن |

heart	qalb	قلب
blood	xun	خون
brain	maqz	مغز
nerve	asab	عصب

bone	ostexān	استخوان
skeleton	eskelet	اسکلت
spine (backbone)	sotun-e faqarāt	ستون فقرات
rib	dande	دنده
skull	jomjome	جمجمه

muscle	azole	عضله
lungs	rie	ریه
skin	pust	پوست

head	sar	سر
face	surat	صورت
nose	bini	بینی
forehead	pišāni	پیشانی
cheek	gune	گونه

mouth	dahān	دهان
tongue	zabān	زبان
tooth	dandān	دندان
lips	lab-hā	لب ها
chin	čāne	چانه

ear	guš	گوش
neck	gardan	گردن
throat	galu	گلو

eye	češm	چشم
pupil	mardomak	مردمک
eyebrow	abru	ابرو
eyelash	može	مژه

hair	mu-hā	مو ها
hairstyle	model-e mu	مدل مو
mustache	sebil	سبیل
beard	riš	ریش
to have (a beard, etc.)	gozāštan	گذاشتن
bald (adj)	tās	طاس

hand	dast	دست
arm	bāzu	بازو
finger	angošt	انگشت
nail	nāxon	ناخن
palm	kaf-e dast	کف دست

shoulder	ketf	کتف
leg	pā	پا
foot	pā	پا

| knee | zānu | زانو |
| heel | pāšne-ye pā | پاشنهٔ پا |

back	pošt	پشت
waist	dur-e kamar	دور کمر
beauty mark	xāl	خال
birthmark (café au lait spot)	xāl-e mādarzād	خال مادرزاد

5. Medicine. Diseases. Drugs

health	salāmati	سلامتی
well (not sick)	sālem	سالم
sickness	bimāri	بیماری
to be sick	bimār budan	بیمار بودن
ill, sick (adj)	bimār	بیمار

cold (illness)	sarmā xordegi	سرما خوردگی
to catch a cold	sarmā xordan	سرما خوردن
tonsillitis	varam-e lowze	ورم لوزه
pneumonia	zātorrie	ذات الریه
flu, influenza	ānfolānzā	آنفولانزا

runny nose (coryza)	āb-e rizeš-e bini	آب ریزش بینی
cough	sorfe	سرفه
to cough (vi)	sorfe kardan	سرفه کردن
to sneeze (vi)	atse kardan	عطسه کردن

stroke	sekte-ye maqzi	سکته مغزی
heart attack	sekte-ye qalbi	سکته قلبی
allergy	ālerži	آلرژی
asthma	āsm	آسم
diabetes	diyābet	دیابت

tumor	tumor	تومور
cancer	saratān	سرطان
alcoholism	alkolism	الکلیسم
AIDS	eydz	ایدز
fever	tab	تب
seasickness	daryā-zadegi	دریازدگی

bruise (hématome)	kabudi	کبودی
bump (lump)	barāmadegi	برآمدگی
to limp (vi)	langidan	لنگیدن
dislocation	dar raftegi	دررفتگی
to dislocate (vt)	dar raftan	دررفتن

fracture	šekastegi	شکستگی
burn (injury)	suxtegi	سوختگی
injury	zaxm	زخم

| pain, ache | dard | درد |
| toothache | dandān-e dard | دندان درد |

to sweat (perspire)	araq kardan	عرق کردن
deaf (adj)	kar	کر
mute (adj)	lāl	لال

immunity	masuniyat	مصونیت
virus	virus	ویروس
microbe	mikrob	میکروب
bacterium	bākteri	باکتری
infection	ofunat	عفونت

hospital	bimārestān	بیمارستان
cure	mo'āleje	معالجه
to vaccinate (vt)	vāksine kardan	واکسینه کردن
to be in a coma	dar komā budan	در کما بودن
intensive care	morāqebat-e viže	مراقبت ویژه
symptom	alāem-e bimāri	علائم بیماری
pulse	nabz	نبض

6. Feelings. Emotions. Conversation

I, me	man	من
you	to	تو
he, she, it	u	او

we	mā	ما
you (to a group)	šomā	شما
they	ān-hā	آنها

Hello! (form.)	salām	سلام
Good morning!	sobh bexeyr	صبح بخیر
Good afternoon!	ruz bexeyr!	روز بخیر!
Good evening!	asr bexeyr	عصربخیر

to say hello	salām kardan	سلام کردن
to greet (vt)	salām kardan	سلام کردن
How are you? (form.)	haletān četowr ast?	حالتان چطور است؟
How are you? (fam.)	četorid?	چطورید؟
Goodbye!	xodāhāfez	خداحافظ
Bye!	bāy bāy	بای بای
Thank you!	motešakker-am!	متشکرم!

feelings	ehsāsat	احساسات
to be hungry	gorosne budan	گرسنه بودن
to be thirsty	tešne budan	تشنه بودن
tired (adj)	xaste	خسته
to be worried	negarān šodan	نگران شدن
to be nervous	asabi šodan	عصبی شدن

| hope | omid | امید |
| to hope (vi, vt) | omid dāštan | امید داشتن |

character	šaxsiyat	شخصیت
modest (adj)	forutan	فروتن
lazy (adj)	tanbal	تنبل
generous (adj)	ba sexāvat	با سخاوت
talented (adj)	bā este'dād	با استعداد

honest (adj)	sādeq	صادق
serious (adj)	jeddi	جدی
shy, timid (adj)	xejālati	خجالتی
sincere (adj)	sādeq	صادق
coward	tarsu	ترسو

to sleep (vi)	xābidan	خوابیدن
dream	royā	رویا
bed	taxt-e xāb	تخت خواب
pillow	bālešt	بالشت

insomnia	bi-xābi	بیخوابی
to go to bed	be raxtexāb raftan	به رختخواب رفتن
nightmare	kābus	کابوس
alarm clock	sā'at-e zang dār	ساعت زنگ دار

smile	labxand	لبخند
to smile (vi)	labxand zadan	لبخند زدن
to laugh (vi)	xandidan	خندیدن

quarrel	da'vā	دعوا
insult	towhin	توهین
resentment	ranješ	رنجش
angry (mad)	xašmgin	خشمگین

7. Clothing. Personal accessories

clothes	lebās	لباس
coat (overcoat)	pāltow	پالتو
fur coat	pālto-ye pustin	پالتوی پوستین
jacket (e.g., leather ~)	kot	کت
raincoat (trenchcoat, etc.)	bārāni	بارانی

shirt (button shirt)	pirāhan	پیراهن
pants	šalvār	شلوار
suit jacket	kot	کت
suit	kat-o šalvār	کت و شلوار

dress (frock)	lebās	لباس
skirt	dāman	دامن
T-shirt	tey šarr-at	تی شرت

bathrobe	howle-ye hamām	حوله حمام
pajamas	pižāme	پیژامه
workwear	lebās-e kār	لباس کار
underwear	lebās-e zir	لباس زیر
socks	jurāb	جوراب
bra	sine-ye band	سینه بند
pantyhose	jurāb-e šalvāri	جوراب شلواری
stockings (thigh highs)	jurāb-e sāqeboland	جوراب ساقه بلند
bathing suit	māyo	مایو
hat	kolāh	کلاه
footwear	kafš	کفش
boots (e.g., cowboy ~)	čakme	چکمه
heel	pāšne-ye kafš	پاشنهٔ کفش
shoestring	band-e kafš	بند کفش
shoe polish	vāks	واکس
cotton (n)	panbe	پنبه
wool (n)	pašm	پشم
fur (n)	xaz	خز
gloves	dastkeš	دستکش
mittens	dastkeš-e yek angošti	دستکش یک انگشتی
scarf (muffler)	šāl-e gardan	شال گردن
glasses (eyeglasses)	eynak	عینک
umbrella	čatr	چتر
tie (necktie)	kerāvāt	کراوات
handkerchief	dastmāl	دستمال
comb	šāne	شانه
hairbrush	bores-e mu	برس مو
buckle	sagak	سگک
belt	kamarband	کمربند
purse	keyf-e zanāne	کیف زنانه
collar	yaqe	یقه
pocket	jib	جیب
sleeve	āstin	آستین
fly (on trousers)	zip	زیپ
zipper (fastener)	zip	زیپ
button	dokme	دکمه
to get dirty (vi)	kasif šodan	کثیف شدن
stain (mark, spot)	lakke	لکه

8. City. Urban institutions

store	maqāze	مغازه
shopping mall	markaz-e tejāri	مرکز تجاری

supermarket	supermārket	سوپرمارکت
shoe store	kafš foruši	کفش فروشی
bookstore	ketāb-foruši	کتاب فروشی
drugstore, pharmacy	dāruxāne	داروخانه
bakery	nānvāyi	نانوایی
pastry shop	qannādi	قنادی
grocery store	baqqāli	بقالی
butcher shop	gušt foruši	گوشت فروشی
produce store	sabzi foruši	سبزی فروشی
market	bāzār	بازار
hair salon	ārāyešgāh	آرایشگاه
post office	post	پست
dry cleaners	xošk-šuyi	خشک‌شویی
circus	sirak	سیرک
zoo	bāq-e vahš	باغ وحش
theater	teātr	تئاتر
movie theater	sinamā	سینما
museum	muze	موزه
library	ketābxāne	کتابخانه
mosque	masjed	مسجد
synagogue	kenešt	کنشت
cathedral	kelisā-ye jāme'	کلیسای جامع
temple	ma'bad	معبد
church	kelisā	کلیسا
college	anistito	انستیتو
university	dānešgāh	دانشگاه
school	madrese	مدرسه
hotel	hotel	هتل
bank	bānk	بانک
embassy	sefārat	سفارت
travel agency	āžāns-e jahāngardi	آژانس جهانگردی
subway	metro	مترو
hospital	bimārestān	بیمارستان
gas station	pomp-e benzin	پمپ بنزین
parking lot	pārking	پارکینگ
ENTRANCE	vorud	ورود
EXIT	xoruj	خروج
PUSH	hel dādan	هل دادن
PULL	bekešid	بکشید
OPEN	bāz	باز
CLOSED	baste	بسته
monument	mojassame	مجسمه
fortress	qal'e	قلعه

palace	kāx	کاخ
medieval (adj)	qorun-e vasati	قرون وسطی
ancient (adj)	qadimi	قدیمی
national (adj)	melli	ملی
famous (monument, etc.)	mašhur	مشهور

9. Money. Finances

money	pul	پول
coin	sekke	سکه
dollar	dolār	دلار
euro	yuro	یورو
ATM	xodpardāz	خودپرداز
currency exchange	sarrāfi	صرافی
exchange rate	nerx-e arz	نرخ ارز
cash	pul-e naqd	پول نقد
How much?	čeqadr?	چقدر؟
to pay (vi, vt)	pardāxtan	پرداختن
payment	pardāxt	پرداخت
change (give the ~)	pul-e xerad	پول خرد
price	qeymat	قیمت
discount	taxfif	تخفیف
cheap (adj)	arzān	ارزان
expensive (adj)	gerān	گران
bank	bānk	بانک
account	hesāb-e bānki	حساب بانکی
credit card	kārt-e e'tebāri	کارت اعتباری
check	ček	چک
to write a check	ček neveštan	چک نوشتن
checkbook	daste-ye ček	دسته چک
debt	qarz	قرض
debtor	bedehkār	بدهکار
to lend (money)	qarz dādan	قرض دادن
to borrow (vi, vt)	qarz gereftan	قرض گرفتن
to rent (~ a tuxedo)	kerāye kardan	کرایه کردن
on credit (adv)	xarid-e e'tebāri	خرید اعتباری
wallet	kif-e pul	کیف پول
safe	gāvsanduq	گاوصندوق
inheritance	mirās	میراث
fortune (wealth)	dārāyi	دارایی
tax	māliyāt	مالیات
fine	jarime	جریمه
to fine (vt)	jarime kardan	جریمه کردن

T&P Books. English-Persian phrasebook & concise dictionary

wholesale (adj)	omde	عمده
retail (adj)	xorde-foruši	خرده فروشی
to insure (vt)	bime kardan	بیمه کردن
insurance	bime	بیمه
capital	sarmāye	سرمایه
turnover	gardeš mo'āmelāt	گردش معاملات
stock (share)	sahām	سهام
profit	sud	سود
profitable (adj)	sudāvar	سودآور
crisis	bohrān	بحران
bankruptcy	varšekastegi	ورشکستگی
to go bankrupt	varšekast šodan	ورشکست شدن
accountant	hesābdār	حسابدار
salary	hoquq	حقوق
bonus (money)	pādāš	پاداش

10. Transportation

bus	otobus	اتوبوس
streetcar	terāmvā	تراموا
trolley bus	otobus-e barqi	اتوبوس برقی
to go by ...	raftan bā	رفتن با
to get on (~ the bus)	savār šodan	سوار شدن
to get off ...	piyāde šodan	پیاده شدن
stop (e.g., bus ~)	istgāh-e otobus	ایستگاه اتوبوس
terminus	istgāh-e āxar	ایستگاه آخر
schedule	barnāme	برنامه
ticket	belit	بلیط
to be late (for ...)	ta'xir dāštan	تأخیرداشتن
taxi, cab	tāksi	تاکسی
by taxi	bā tāksi	با تاکسی
taxi stand	istgāh-e tāksi	ایستگاه تاکسی
traffic	obur-o morur	عبور و مرور
rush hour	sā'at-e šoluqi	ساعت شلوغی
to park (vi)	pārk kardan	پارک کردن
subway	metro	مترو
station	istgāh	ایستگاه
train	qatār	قطار
train station	istgāh-e rāh-e āhan	ایستگاه راه آهن
rails	reyl-hā	ریل ها
compartment	kupe	کوپه
berth	taxt-e kupe	تخت کوپه

airplane	havāpeymā	هواپیما
air ticket	belit-e havāpeymā	بلیط هواپیما
airline	šerkat-e havāpeymāyi	شرکت هواپیمایی
airport	forudgāh	فرودگاه
flight (act of flying)	parvāz	پرواز
luggage	bār	بار
luggage cart	čarx-e hamle bar	چرخ حمل بار
ship	kešti	کشتی
cruise ship	kešti-ye tafrihi	کشتی تفریحی
yacht	qāyeq-e tafrihi	قایق تفریحی
boat (flat-bottomed ~)	qāyeq	قایق
captain	kāpitān	کاپیتان
cabin	otāq-e kešti	اتاق کشتی
port (harbor)	bandar	بندر
bicycle	dočarxe	دوچرخه
scooter	eskuter	اسکوتر
motorcycle, bike	motorsiklet	موتورسیکلت
pedal	pedāl	پدال
pump	pomp	پمپ
wheel	čarx	چرخ
automobile, car	otomobil	اتومبیل
ambulance	āmbolāns	آمبولانس
truck	kāmiyon	کامیون
used (adj)	dast-e dovvom	دست دوم
car crash	tasādof	تصادف
repair	ta'mir	تعمیر

11. Food. Part 1

meat	gušt	گوشت
chicken	morq	مرغ
duck	ordak	اردک
pork	gušt-e xuk	گوشت خوک
veal	gušt-e gusāle	گوشت گوساله
lamb	gušt-e gusfand	گوشت گوسفند
beef	gušt-e gāv	گوشت گاو
sausage (bologna, pepperoni, etc.)	kālbās	کالباس
egg	toxm-e morq	تخم مرغ
fish	māhi	ماهی
cheese	panir	پنیر
sugar	qand	قند
salt	namak	نمک

rice	berenj	برنج
pasta (macaroni)	mākāroni	ماکارونی
butter	kare	کره
vegetable oil	rowqan-e nabāti	روغن نباتی
bread	nān	نان
chocolate (n)	šokolāt	شکلات
wine	šarāb	شراب
coffee	qahve	قهوه
milk	šir	شیر
juice	āb-e mive	آب میوه
beer	ābejow	آبجو
tea	čāy	چای
tomato	gowje farangi	گوجه فرنگی
cucumber	xiyār	خیار
carrot	havij	هویج
potato	sib zamini	سیب زمینی
onion	piyāz	پیاز
garlic	sir	سیر
cabbage	kalam	کلم
beetroot	čoqondar	چغندر
eggplant	bādenjān	بادنجان
dill	šavid	شوید
lettuce	kāhu	کاهو
corn (maize)	zorrat	ذرت
fruit	mive	میوه
apple	sib	سیب
pear	golābi	گلابی
lemon	limu	لیمو
orange	porteqāl	پرتقال
strawberry (garden ~)	tut-e farangi	توت فرنگی
plum	ālu	آلو
raspberry	tamešk	تمشک
pineapple	ānānās	آناناس
banana	mowz	موز
watermelon	hendevāne	هندوانه
grape	angur	انگور
melon	xarboze	خربزه

12. Food. Part 2

cuisine	qazā	غذا
recipe	dastur-e poxt	دستور پخت
food	qazā	غذا
to have breakfast	sobhāne xordan	صبحانه خوردن
to have lunch	nāhār xordan	ناهار خوردن

to have dinner	šām xordan	شام خوردن
taste, flavor	maze	مزه
tasty (adj)	xoš mazze	خوش مزه
cold (adj)	sard	سرد
hot (adj)	dāq	داغ
sweet (sugary)	širin	شیرین
salty (adj)	šur	شور
sandwich (bread)	sāndevič	ساندویچ
side dish	moxallafāt	مخلفات
filling (for cake, pie)	čāšni	چاشنی
sauce	ses	سس
piece (of cake, pie)	tekke	تکه
diet	režim	رژیم
vitamin	vitāmin	ویتامین
calorie	kālori	کالری
vegetarian (n)	giyāh xār	گیاه خوار
restaurant	resturān	رستوران
coffee house	kāfe	کافه
appetite	eštehā	اشتها
Enjoy your meal!	nuš-e jān	نوش جان
waiter	pišxedmat	پیشخدمت
waitress	pišxedmat	پیشخدمت
bartender	motesaddi-ye bār	متصدی بار
menu	meno	منو
spoon	qāšoq	قاشق
knife	kārd	کارد
fork	čangāl	چنگال
cup (e.g., coffee ~)	fenjān	فنجان
plate (dinner ~)	bošqāb	بشقاب
saucer	na'lbeki	نعلبکی
napkin (on table)	dastmāl	دستمال
toothpick	xelāl-e dandān	خلال دندان
to order (meal)	sefāreš dādan	سفارش دادن
course, dish	qazā	غذا
portion	pors	پرس
appetizer	piš qazā	پیش غذا
salad	sālād	سالاد
soup	sup	سوپ
dessert	deser	دسر
jam (whole fruit jam)	morabbā	مربا
ice-cream	bastani	بستنی
check	surat hesāb	صورت حساب
to pay the check	surat-e hesāb rā pardāxtan	صورت حساب را پرداختن
tip	an'ām	انعام

13. House. Apartment. Part 1

house	xāne	خانه
country house	xāne-ye xārej-e šahr	خانهٔ خارج شهر
villa (seaside ~)	vilā	ویلا
floor, story	tabaqe	طبقه
entrance	darb-e vorudi	درب ورودی
wall	divār	دیوار
roof	bām	بام
chimney	dudkeš	دودکش
attic (storage place)	zir-širvāni	زیرشیروانی
window	panjere	پنجره
window ledge	tāqče-ye panjare	طاقچهٔ پنجره
balcony	bālkon	بالکن
stairs (stairway)	pellekān	پلکان
mailbox	sanduq-e post	صندوق پست
garbage can	zobāle dān	زباله دان
elevator	āsānsor	آسانسور
electricity	barq	برق
light bulb	lāmp	لامپ
switch	kelid	کلید
wall socket	periz	پریز
fuse	fiyuz	فیوز
door	darb	درب
handle, doorknob	dastgire-ye dar	دستگیرهٔ در
key	kelid	کلید
doormat	pādari	پادری
door lock	qofl	قفل
doorbell	zang-e dar	زنگ در
knock (at the door)	dar zadan	درزدن
to knock (vi)	dar zadan	درزدن
peephole	češmi	چشمی
yard	hayāt	حیاط
garden	bāq	باغ
swimming pool	estaxr	استخر
gym (home gym)	sālon-e varzeš	سالن ورزش
tennis court	zamin-e tenis	زمین تنیس
garage	gārāž	گاراژ
private property	melk-e xosusi	ملک خصوصی
warning sign	alāmat-e hošdār	علامت هشدار
security	hefāzat	حفاظت
security guard	negahbān	نگهبان
renovations	ta'mir	تعمیر

to renovate (vt)	ta'mir kardan	تعمیر کردن
to put in order	morattab kardan	مرتب کردن
to paint (~ a wall)	rang kardan	رنگ کردن
wallpaper	kāqaz-e divāri	کاغذ دیواری
to varnish (vt)	lāk zadan	لاک زدن
pipe	lule	لوله
tools	abzār	ابزار
basement	zirzamin	زیرزمین
sewerage (system)	fāzelāb	فاضلاب

14. House. Apartment. Part 2

apartment	āpārtemān	آپارتمان
room	otāq	اتاق
bedroom	otāq-e xāb	اتاق خواب
dining room	otāq-e qazāxori	اتاق غذاخوری
living room	mehmānxāne	مهمانخانه
study (home office)	daftar	دفتر
entry room	tālār-e vorudi	تالار ورودی
bathroom (room with a bath or shower)	hammām	حمام
half bath	tuālet	توالت
floor	kaf	کف
ceiling	saqf	سقف
to dust (vt)	gardgiri kardan	گردگیری کردن
vacuum cleaner	jāru barqi	جارو برقی
to vacuum (vt)	jāru barq-i kešidan	جارو برقی کشیدن
mop	jāru-ye dastedār	جاروی دسته دار
dust cloth	kohne	کهنه
short broom	jārub	جاروب
dustpan	xāk andāz	خاک انداز
furniture	mobl	مبل
table	miz	میز
chair	sandali	صندلی
armchair	mobl-e rāhati	مبل راحتی
bookcase	qafase-ye ketāb	قفسه کتاب
shelf	qafase	قفسه
wardrobe	komod	کمد
mirror	āyene	آینه
carpet	farš	فرش
fireplace	šumine	شومینه
drapes	parde	پرده

table lamp	čerāq-e rumizi	چراغ رومیزی
chandelier	luster	لوستر
kitchen	āšpazxāne	آشپزخانه
gas stove (range)	ojāgh-e gāz	اجاق گاز
electric stove	ojāgh-e barghi	اجاق برقی
microwave oven	māykrofer	مایکروفر
refrigerator	yaxčāl	یخچال
freezer	fereyzer	فریزر
dishwasher	māšin-e zarfšuyi	ماشین ظرفشویی
faucet	šir	شیر
meat grinder	čarx-e gušt	چرخ گوشت
juicer	ābmive giri	آبمیوه گیری
toaster	towster	توستر
mixer	maxlut kon	مخلوط کن
coffee machine	qahve sāz	قهوه ساز
kettle	ketri	کتری
teapot	quri	قوری
TV set	televiziyon	تلویزیون
VCR (video recorder)	video	ویدئو
iron (e.g., steam ~)	oto	اتو
telephone	telefon	تلفن

15. Professions. Social status

director	modir	مدیر
superior	māfowq	مافوق
president	ra'is jomhur	رئیس جمهور
assistant	mo'āven	معاون
secretary	monši	منشی
owner, proprietor	sāheb	صاحب
partner	šarik	شریک
stockholder	sahāmdār	سهامدار
businessman	bāzargān	بازرگان
millionaire	milyuner	میلیونر
billionaire	milyārder	میلیاردر
actor	bāzigar	بازیگر
architect	me'mār	معمار
banker	kārmand-e bānk	کارمند بانک
broker	dallāl-e kārgozār	دلال کارگزار
veterinarian	dāmpezešk	دامپزشک
doctor	pezešk	پزشک

chambermaid	mostaxdem	مستخدم
designer	tarāh	طراح
correspondent	xabarnegār	خبرنگار
delivery man	peyk	پیک
electrician	barq-e kār	برق کار
musician	muzisiyan	موزیسین
babysitter	parastār bače	پرستار بچه
hairdresser	ārāyešgar	آرایشگر
herder, shepherd	čupān	چوپان
singer (masc.)	xānande	خواننده
translator	motarjem	مترجم
writer	nevisande	نویسنده
carpenter	najjār	نجار
cook	āšpaz	آشپز
fireman	ātaš nešān	آتش نشان
police officer	polis	پلیس
mailman	nāme resān	نامه رسان
programmer	barnāme-ye nevis	برنامه نویس
salesman (store staff)	forušande	فروشنده
worker	kārgar	کارگر
gardener	bāqbān	باغبان
plumber	lule keš	لوله کش
dentist	dandān pezešk	دندان پزشک
flight attendant (fem.)	mehmāndār-e havāpeymā	مهماندار هواپیما
dancer (masc.)	raqqās	رقاص
bodyguard	mohāfez-e šaxsi	محافظ شخصی
scientist	dānešmand	دانشمند
schoolteacher	mo'allem	معلم
farmer	kešāvarz	کشاورز
surgeon	jarrāh	جراح
miner	ma'danči	معدنچی
chef (kitchen chef)	sarāšpaz	سرآشپز
driver	rānande	راننده

16. Sport

kind of sports	anvā-e varzeš	انواع ورزش
soccer	futbāl	فوتبال
hockey	hāki	هاکی
basketball	basketbāl	بسکتبال
baseball	beysbāl	بیسبال
volleyball	vālibāl	والیبال
boxing	boks	بوکس

wrestling	kešti	کشتی
tennis	tenis	تنیس
swimming	šenā	شنا

chess	šatranj	شطرنج
running	do	دو
athletics	varzeš	ورزش
figure skating	raqs ruy yax	رقص روی یخ
cycling	dočarxe savāri	دوچرخه سواری

billiards	bilyārd	بیلیارد
bodybuilding	badansāzi	بدنسازی
golf	golf	گلف
scuba diving	dāyving	دایوینگ
sailing	qāyeq-rāni bādbani	قایق رانی بادبانی
archery	tirandāzi bā kamān	تیراندازی با کمان

period, half	nime	نیمه
half-time	hāf tāym	هاف تایم
tie	mosāvi	مساوی
to tie (vi)	bāzi rā mosāvi kardan	بازی رامساوی کردن

treadmill	pist-e do	پیست دو
player	bāzikon	بازیکن
substitute	bāzikon-e zaxire	بازیکن ذخیره
substitutes bench	nimkat-e zaxire	نیمکت ذخیره

match	mosābeqe	مسابقه
goal	darvāze	دروازه
goalkeeper	darvāze bān	دروازه بان
goal (score)	gol	گل

Olympic Games	bāzihā-ye olampik	بازی‌های المپیک
to set a record	rekord gozāštan	رکورد گذاشتن
final	fināl	فینال
champion	qahremān	قهرمان
championship	mosābeqe-ye qahremāni	مسابقه قهرمانی

winner	barande	برنده
victory	piruzi	پیروزی
to win (vi)	piruz šodan	پیروز شدن
to lose (not win)	bāxtan	باختن
medal	medāl	مدال

first place	rotbe-ye avval	رتبه اول
second place	rotbe-ye dovvom	رتبه دوم
third place	rotbe-ye sevvom	رتبه سوم

stadium	varzešgāh	ورزشگاه
fan, supporter	tarafdār	طرفدار
trainer, coach	morabbi	مربی
training	tamrin	تمرین

17. Foreign languages. Orthography

language	zabān	زبان
to study (vt)	dars xāndan	درس خواندن
pronunciation	talaffoz	تلفظ
accent	lahje	لهجه
noun	esm	اسم
adjective	sefat	صفت
verb	fe'l	فعل
adverb	qeyd	قید
pronoun	zamir	ضمیر
interjection	harf-e nedā	حرف ندا
preposition	harf-e ezāfe	حرف اضافه
root	riše-ye kalame	ریشه کلمه
ending	pasvand	پسوند
prefix	pišvand	پیشوند
syllable	hejā	هجا
suffix	pasvand	پسوند
stress mark	fešar-e hejā	فشار هجا
period, dot	noqte	نقطه
comma	virgul	ویرگول
colon	donoqte	دونقطه
ellipsis	čand noqte	چند نقطه
question	soāl	سؤال
question mark	alāmat-e soāl	علامت سؤال
exclamation point	alāmat-e taajjob	علامت تعجب
in quotation marks	dar giyume	در گیومه
in parenthesis	dar parāntez	در پرانتز
letter	harf	حرف
capital letter	harf-e bozorg	حرف بزرگ
sentence	jomle	جمله
group of words	ebārat	عبارت
expression	bayān	بیان
subject	nahād	نهاد
predicate	gozāre	گزاره
line	satr	سطر
paragraph	band	بند
synonym	moterādef	مترادف
antonym	motezād	متضاد
exception	estesnā	استثنا
to underline (vt)	xatt kešidan	خط کشیدن
rules	qavā'ed	قواعد

grammar	gerāmer	گرامر
vocabulary	vājegān	واژگان
phonetics	āvā-šenāsi	آواشناسی
alphabet	alefbā	الفبا

textbook	ketāb-e darsi	کتاب درسی
dictionary	farhang-e loqat	فرهنگ لغت
phrasebook	ketāb-e mokāleme	کتاب مکالمه

word	kalame	کلمه
meaning	ma'ni	معنی
memory	hāfeze	حافظه

18. The Earth. Geography

the Earth	zamin	زمین
the globe (the Earth)	kare-ye zamin	کرۀ زمین
planet	sayyāre	سیاره

geography	joqrāfiyā	جغرافیا
nature	tabi'at	طبیعت
map	naqše	نقشه
atlas	atlas	اطلس

in the north	dar šomāl	در شمال
in the south	dar jonub	در جنوب
in the west	dar qarb	در غرب
in the east	dar šarq	در شرق

sea	daryā	دریا
ocean	oqyānus	اقیانوس
gulf (bay)	xalij	خلیج
straits	tange	تنگه

continent (mainland)	qāre	قاره
island	jazire	جزیره
peninsula	šeb-e jazire	شبه جزیره
archipelago	majma'-ol-jazāyer	مجمع‌الجزایر

harbor	langargāh	لنگرگاه
coral reef	tappe-ye marjāni	تپه مرجانی
shore	sāhel	ساحل
coast	sāhel	ساحل

| flow (flood tide) | mod | مد |
| ebb (ebb tide) | jazr | جزر |

latitude	arz-e joqrāfiyāyi	عرض جغرافیایی
longitude	tul-e joqrāfiyāyi	طول جغرافیایی
parallel	movāzi	موازی

equator	xatt-e ostavā	خط استوا
sky	āsemān	آسمان
horizon	ofoq	افق
atmosphere	jav	جو

mountain	kuh	کوه
summit, top	qolle	قله
cliff	saxre	صخره
hill	tappe	تپه

volcano	ātaš-fešān	آتشفشان
glacier	yaxčāl	يخچال
waterfall	ābšār	آبشار
plain	jolge	جلگه

river	rudxāne	رودخانه
spring (natural source)	češme	چشمه
bank (of river)	sāhel	ساحل
downstream (adv)	be samt-e pāin-e rudxāne	به سمت پائين رودخانه
upstream (adv)	be samt-e bālā-ye rudxāne	به سمت بالای رودخانه

lake	daryāče	درياچه
dam	sad	سد
canal	kānāl	کانال
swamp (marshland)	bātlāq	باتلاق
ice	yax	يخ

19. Countries of the world. Part 1

Europe	orupā	اروپا
European Union	ettehādiye-ye orupā	اتحادیه اروپا
European (n)	orupāyi	اروپایی
European (adj)	orupāyi	اروپایی

Austria	otriš	اتریش
Great Britain	beritāniyā-ye kabir	بریتانیای کبیر
England	engelestān	انگلستان
Belgium	belžik	بلژیک
Germany	ālmān	آلمان

Netherlands	holand	هلند
Holland	holand	هلند
Greece	yunān	یونان
Denmark	dānmārk	دانمارک
Ireland	irland	ایرلند

Iceland	island	ایسلند
Spain	espāniyā	اسپانیا
Italy	itāliyā	ایتالیا
Cyprus	qebres	قبرس

Malta	mält	مالت
Norway	norvež	نروژ
Portugal	porteqāl	پرتغال
Finland	fanländ	فنلاند
France	farānse	فرانسه
Sweden	sued	سوئد

Switzerland	suis	سوئیس
Scotland	eskätland	اسکاتلند
Vatican	vätikān	واتیکان
Liechtenstein	lixteneštāyn	لیختنااشتاین
Luxembourg	lokzāmborg	لوکزامبورگ

Monaco	monāko	موناکو
Albania	ālbāni	آلبانی
Bulgaria	bolqārestān	بلغارستان
Hungary	majārestān	مجارستان
Latvia	letuni	لتونی

Lithuania	litvāni	لیتوانی
Poland	lahestān	لهستان
Romania	romāni	رومانی
Serbia	serbestān	صربستان
Slovakia	eslovāki	اسلواکی

Croatia	korovāsi	کرواسی
Czech Republic	jomhuri-ye ček	جمهوری چک
Estonia	estoni	استونی
Bosnia and Herzegovina	bosni-yo herzogovin	بوسنی وهرزگوین
Macedonia (Republic of ~)	jomhuri-ye maqduniye	جمهوری مقدونیه

Slovenia	eslovoni	اسلوونی
Montenegro	montenegro	مونته‌نگرو
Belarus	belārus	بلاروس
Moldova, Moldavia	moldāvi	مولداوی
Russia	rusiye	روسیه
Ukraine	okrāyn	اوکراین

20. Countries of the world. Part 2

Asia	āsiyā	آسیا
Vietnam	viyetnām	ویتنام
India	hendustān	هندوستان
Israel	esrāil	اسرائیل
China	čin	چین

Lebanon	lobnān	لبنان
Mongolia	moqolestān	مغولستان
Malaysia	mālezi	مالزی
Pakistan	pākestān	پاکستان

Saudi Arabia	arabestān-e so'udi	عربستان سعودی
Thailand	tāyland	تایلند
Taiwan	tāyvān	تایوان
Turkey	torkiye	ترکیه
Japan	žāpon	ژاپن
Afghanistan	afqānestān	افغانستان
Bangladesh	bangelādeš	بنگلادش
Indonesia	andonezi	اندونزی
Jordan	ordon	اردن
Iraq	arāq	عراق
Iran	irān	ایران
Cambodia	kāmboj	کامبوج
Kuwait	koveyt	کویت
Laos	lāus	لائوس
Myanmar	miyānmār	میانمار
Nepal	nepāl	نپال
United Arab Emirates	emārāt-e mottahede-ye arabi	امارات متحده عربی
Syria	suriye	سوریه
Palestine	felestin	فلسطین
South Korea	kare-ye jonubi	کرۀ جنوبی
North Korea	kare-ye šomāli	کرۀ شمالی
United States of America	eyālāt-e mottahede-ye emrikā	ایالات متحدۀ امریکا
Canada	kānādā	کانادا
Mexico	mekzik	مکزیک
Argentina	āržāntin	آرژانتین
Brazil	berezil	برزیل
Colombia	kolombiyā	کلمبیا
Cuba	kubā	کوبا
Chile	šhili	شیلی
Venezuela	venezuelā	ونزوئلا
Ecuador	ekvādor	اکوادور
The Bahamas	bāhāmā	باهاما
Panama	pānāmā	پاناما
Egypt	mesr	مصر
Morocco	marākeš	مراکش
Tunisia	tunes	تونس
Kenya	keniyā	کنیا
Libya	libi	لیبی
South Africa	jomhuri-ye āfriqā-ye jonubi	جمهوری آفریقای جنوبی
Australia	ostorāliyā	استرالیا
New Zealand	niyuzland	نیوزلند

21. Weather. Natural disasters

weather	havā	هوا
weather forecast	piš bini havā	پیش بینی هوا
temperature	damā	دما
thermometer	damāsanj	دماسنج
barometer	havāsanj	هواسنج
sun	āftāb	آفتاب
to shine (vi)	tābidan	تابیدن
sunny (day)	āftābi	آفتابی
to come up (vi)	tolu' kardan	طلوع کردن
to set (vi)	qorob kardan	غروب کردن
rain	bārān	باران
it's raining	bārān mibārad	باران می بارد
pouring rain	bārān šodid	باران شدید
rain cloud	abr-e bārānzā	ابر باران زا
puddle	čāle	چاله
to get wet (in rain)	xis šodan	خیس شدن
thunderstorm	tufān	طوفان
lightning (~ strike)	barq	برق
to flash (vi)	barq zadan	برق زدن
thunder	ra'd	رعد
it's thundering	ra'd mizanad	رعد می زند
hail	tagarg	تگرگ
it's hailing	tagarg mibārad	تگرگ می بارد
heat (extreme ~)	garmā	گرما
it's hot	havā xeyli garm ast	هوا خیلی گرم است
it's warm	havā garm ast	هوا گرم است
it's cold	sard ast	سرد است
fog (mist)	meh	مه
foggy	meh ālud	مه آلود
cloud	abr	ابر
cloudy (adj)	abri	ابری
humidity	rotubat	رطوبت
snow	barf	برف
it's snowing	barf mibārad	برف می بارد
frost (severe ~, freezing cold)	yaxbandān	یخبندان
below zero (adv)	zir-e sefr	زیر صفر
hoarfrost	barf-e rize	برف ریزه
bad weather	havā-ye bad	هوای بد
disaster	balā-ye tabi'i	بلای طبیعی
flood, inundation	seyl	سیل
avalanche	bahman	بهمن

earthquake	zamin-larze	زمین لرزه
tremor, quake	tekān	تکان
epicenter	kānun-e zaminlarze	کانون زمین لرزه
eruption	favarān	فوران
lava	godāze	گدازه

twister, tornado	gerdbād	گردباد
hurricane	tufān	طوفان
tsunami	sonāmi	سونامی
cyclone	gerdbād	گردباد

22. Animals. Part 1

| animal | heyvān | حیوان |
| predator | heyvān-e darande | حیوان درنده |

tiger	bebar	ببر
lion	šir	شیر
wolf	gorg	گرگ
fox	rubāh	روباه
jaguar	jagvār	جگوار

lynx	siyāh guš	سیاه گوش
coyote	gorg-e sahrāyi	گرگ صحرایی
jackal	šoqāl	شغال
hyena	kaftār	کفتار

squirrel	sanjāb	سنجاب
hedgehog	xārpošt	خارپشت
rabbit	xarguš	خرگوش
raccoon	rākon	راکون

hamster	muš-e bozorg	موش بزرگ
mole	muš-e kur	موش کور
mouse	muš	موش
rat	muš-e sahrāyi	موش صحرایی
bat	xoffāš	خفاش

beaver	sag-e ābi	سگ آبی
horse	asb	اسب
deer	āhu	آهو
camel	šotor	شتر
zebra	gurexar	گورخر

whale	nahang	نهنگ
seal	fak	فک
walrus	širmāhi	شیرماهی
dolphin	delfin	دلفین
bear	xers	خرس
monkey	meymun	میمون

elephant	fil	فیل
rhinoceros	kargadan	کرگدن
giraffe	zarrāfe	زرافه
hippopotamus	asb-e ābi	اسب آبی
kangaroo	kāngoro	کانگورو
cat	gorbe	گربه
dog	sag	سگ
cow	gāv	گاو
bull	gāv-e nar	گاو نر
sheep (ewe)	gusfand	گوسفند
goat	boz-e mādde	بز ماده
donkey	xar	خر
pig, hog	xuk	خوک
hen (chicken)	morq	مرغ
rooster	xorus	خروس
duck	ordak	اردک
goose	qāz	غاز
turkey (hen)	buqalamun-e māde	بوقلمون ماده
sheepdog	sag-e gele	سگ گله

23. Animals. Part 2

bird	parande	پرنده
pigeon	kabutar	کبوتر
sparrow	gonješk	گنجشک
tit (great tit)	morq-e zanburxār	مرغ زنبورخوار
magpie	zāqi	زاغی
eagle	oqāb	عقاب
hawk	qerqi	قرقی
falcon	šāhin	شاهین
swan	qu	قو
crane	dornā	درنا
stork	lak lak	لک لک
parrot	tuti	طوطی
peacock	tāvus	طاووس
ostrich	šotormorq	شترمرغ
heron	havāsil	حواصیل
nightingale	bolbol	بلبل
swallow	parastu	پرستو
woodpecker	dārkub	دارکوب
cuckoo	fāxte	فاخته
owl	joqd	جغد
penguin	pangoan	پنگوئن

tuna	tan māhi	تن ماهی
trout	māhi-ye qezelālā	ماهی قزل آلا
eel	mārmāhi	مارماهی

shark	kuse-ye māhi	کوسه ماهی
crab	xarčang	خرچنگ
jellyfish	arus-e daryāyi	عروس دریایی
octopus	hašt pā	هشت پا

starfish	setāre-ye daryāyi	ستاره دریایی
sea urchin	xārpošt-e daryāyi	خارپشت دریایی
seahorse	asb-e daryāyi	اسب دریایی
shrimp	meygu	میگو

snake	mār	مار
viper	af'i	افعی
lizard	susmār	سوسمار
iguana	susmār-e deraxti	سوسمار درختی
chameleon	āftāb-parast	آفتاب پرست
scorpion	aqrab	عقرب

turtle	lāk pošt	لاک پشت
frog	qurbāqe	قورباغه
crocodile	temsāh	تمساح

insect, bug	hašare	حشره
butterfly	parvāne	پروانه
ant	murče	مورچه
fly	magas	مگس

mosquito	paše	پشه
beetle	susk	سوسک
bee	zanbur-e asal	زنبور عسل
spider	ankabut	عنکبوت

24. Trees. Plants

tree	deraxt	درخت
birch	tus	توس
oak	balut	بلوط
linden tree	zirfun	زیرفون
aspen	senowbar-e larzān	صنوبر لرزان

maple	afrā	افرا
spruce	senowbar	صنوبر
pine	kāj	کاج
cedar	sedr	سدر

| poplar | sepidār | سپیدار |
| rowan | zabān gonješk-e kuhi | زبان گنجشک کوهی |

| beech | rāš | راش |
| elm | nārvan-e qermez | نارون قرمز |

ash (tree)	zabān-e gonješk	زبان گنجشک
chestnut	šāh balut	شاه بلوط
palm tree	naxl	نخل
bush	bute	بوته
mushroom	qārč	قارچ
poisonous mushroom	qārč-e sammi	قارچ سمی
cep (Boletus edulis)	qārč-e sefid	قارچ سفید
russula	qārč-e tiqe-ye tord	قارچ تیغه ترد
fly agaric	qārč-e magas	قارچ مگس
death cap	kolāhak-e marg	کلاهک مرگ

flower	gol	گل
bouquet (of flowers)	daste-ye gol	دسته گل
rose (flower)	gol-e sorx	گل سرخ
tulip	lāle	لاله
carnation	mixak	میخک

camomile	bābune	بابونه
cactus	kāktus	کاکتوس
lily of the valley	muge	موگه
snowdrop	gol-e barfi	گل برفی
water lily	nilufar-e abi	نیلوفر آبی
greenhouse (tropical ~)	golxāne	گلخانه
lawn	čaman	چمن
flowerbed	baqče-ye gol	باغچه گل

plant	giyāh	گیاه
grass	alaf	علف
leaf	barg	برگ
petal	golbarg	گلبرگ
stem	sāqe	ساقه
young plant (shoot)	javāne	جوانه

cereal crops	qallāt	غلات
wheat	gandom	گندم
rye	čāvdār	چاودار
oats	jow-e sahrāyi	جو صحرایی

millet	arzan	ارزن
barley	jow	جو
corn	zorrat	ذرت
rice	berenj	برنج

25. Various useful words

| balance (of situation) | ta'ādol | تعادل |
| base (basis) | pāye | پایه |

beginning	šoruʻ	شروع
category	tabaqe	طبقه
choice	entexāb	انتخاب
coincidence	tatāboq	تطابق
comparison	qiyās	قیاس
degree (extent, amount)	daraje	درجه
development	pišraft	پیشرفت
difference	farq	فرق
effect (e.g., of drugs)	asar	اثر
effort (exertion)	kušeš	کوشش
element	onsor	عنصر
example (illustration)	mesāl	مثال
fact	haqiqat	حقیقت
help	komak	کمک
ideal	ide āl	ایده آل
kind (sort, type)	noʻ	نوع
mistake, error	eštebāh	اشتباه
moment	lahze	لحظه
obstacle	māneʻ	مانع
part (~ of sth)	joz	جزء
pause (break)	maks	مکث
position	vazʻ	وضع
problem	moškel	مشکل
process	ravand	روند
progress	taraqqi	ترقی
property (quality)	xāsiyat	خاصیت
reaction	vākoneš	واکنش
risk	risk	ریسک
secret	rāz	راز
series	seri	سری
shape (outer form)	šekl	شکل
situation	vazʻiyat	وضعیت
solution	hal	حل
standard (adj)	estāndārd	استاندارد
stop (pause)	tavaqqof	توقف
style	sabok	سبک
system	sistem	سیستم
table (chart)	jadval	جدول
tempo, rate	sorʻat	سرعت
term (word, expression)	estelāh	اصطلاح
truth (e.g., moment of ~)	haqiqat	حقیقت

turn (please wait your ~)	nowbat	نوبت
urgent (adj)	fowri	فوری
utility (usefulness)	fāyede	فایده
variant (alternative)	moteqayyer	متغیر
way (means, method)	tariq	طریق
zone	mantaqe	منطقه

26. Modifiers. Adjectives. Part 1

additional (adj)	ezāfi	اضافی
ancient (~ civilization)	qadimi	قدیمی
artificial (adj)	masnu'i	مصنوعی
bad (adj)	bad	بد
beautiful (person)	zibā	زیبا
big (in size)	bozorg	بزرگ
bitter (taste)	talx	تلخ
blind (sightless)	kur	کور
central (adj)	markazi	مرکزی
children's (adj)	kudakāne	کودکانه
clandestine (secret)	maxfi	مخفی
clean (free from dirt)	pāk	پاک
clever (smart)	bāhuš	باهوش
compatible (adj)	sāzgār	سازگار
contented (satisfied)	rāzi	راضی
dangerous (adj)	xatarnāk	خطرناک
dead (not alive)	morde	مرده
dense (fog, smoke)	qaliz	غلیظ
difficult (decision)	moškel	مشکل
dirty (not clean)	kasif	کثیف
easy (not difficult)	āsān	آسان
empty (glass, room)	xāli	خالی
exact (amount)	daqiq	دقیق
excellent (adj)	āli	عالی
excessive (adj)	ziyād az had	زیاد ازحد
exterior (adj)	xāreji	خارجی
fast (quick)	sari'	سریع
fertile (land, soil)	hāzer	حاصلخیز
fragile (china, glass)	šekanande	شکننده
free (at no cost)	majjāni	مجانی
fresh (~ water)	širin	شیرین
frozen (food)	yax zade	یخ زده
full (completely filled)	por	پر
happy (adj)	xošbaxt	خوشبخت

hard (not soft)	soft	سفت
huge (adj)	bozorg	بزرگ
ill (sick, unwell)	bimār	بیمار
immobile (adj)	bi harekat	بی حرکت
important (adj)	mohem	مهم
interior (adj)	dāxeli	داخلی
last (e.g., ~ week)	piš	پیش
last (final)	āxarin	آخرین
left (e.g., ~ side)	čap	چپ
legal (legitimate)	qānuni	قانونی
light (in weight)	sabok	سبک
liquid (fluid)	māye'	مایع
long (e.g., ~ hair)	derāz	دراز
loud (voice, etc.)	boland	بلند
low (voice)	āheste	آهسته

27. Modifiers. Adjectives. Part 2

main (principal)	asli	اصلی
matt, matte	tār	تار
mysterious (adj)	asrār āmiz	اسرارآرمیز
narrow (street, etc.)	bārik	باریک
native (~ country)	bumi	بومی
negative (~ response)	manfi	منفی
new (adj)	jadid	جدید
next (e.g., ~ week)	digar	دیگر
normal (adj)	ma'muli	معمولی
not difficult (adj)	āsān	آسان
obligatory (adj)	ejbāri	اجباری
old (house)	qadimi	قدیمی
open (adj)	bāz	باز
opposite (adj)	moqābel	مقابل
ordinary (usual)	ādi	عادی
original (unusual)	orijināl	اوریژینال
personal (adj)	xosusi	خصوصی
polite (adj)	moaddab	مؤدب
poor (not rich)	faqir	فقیر
possible (adj)	ehtemāli	احتمالی
principal (main)	asāsi	اساسی
probable (adj)	mohtamel	محتمل
prolonged (e.g., ~ applause)	tulāni	طولانی
public (open to all)	omumi	عمومی
rare (adj)	nāder	نادر

raw (uncooked)	xām	خام
right (not left)	rāst	راست
ripe (fruit)	reside	رسیده
risky (adj)	xatarnāk	خطرناک
sad (~ look)	anduhgin	اندوهگین
second hand (adj)	dast-e dovvom	دست دوم
shallow (water)	kam omq	کم عمق
sharp (blade, etc.)	tiz	تیز
short (in length)	kutāh	کوتاه
similar (adj)	šabih	شبیه
small (in size)	kučak	کوچک
smooth (surface)	hamvār	هموار
soft (~ toys)	narm	نرم
solid (~ wall)	mohkam	محکم
sour (flavor, taste)	torš	ترش
spacious (house, etc.)	vasi'	وسیع
special (adj)	maxsus	مخصوص
straight (line, road)	rāst	راست
strong (person)	nirumand	نیرومند
stupid (foolish)	ahmaq	احمق
superb, perfect (adj)	āli	عالی
sweet (sugary)	širin	شیرین
tan (adj)	boronze	برنزه
tasty (delicious)	xoš mazze	خوش مزه
unclear (adj)	nāmo'ayyan	نامعین

28. Verbs. Part 1

to accuse (vt)	mottaham kardan	متهم کردن
to agree (say yes)	movāfeqat kardan	موافقت کردن
to announce (vt)	e'lām kardan	اعلام کردن
to answer (vi, vt)	javāb dādan	جواب دادن
to apologize (vi)	ozr xāstan	عذر خواستن
to arrive (vi)	residan	رسیدن
to ask (~ oneself)	porsidan	پرسیدن
to be absent	qāyeb budan	غایب بودن
to be afraid	tarsidan	ترسیدن
to be born	motevalled šodan	متولد شدن
to be in a hurry	ajale kardan	عجله کردن
to beat (to hit)	zadan	زدن
to begin (vt)	šoru' kardan	شروع کردن
to believe (in God)	e'teqād dāštan	اعتقاد داشتن
to belong to …	ta'alloq dāštan	تعلق داشتن

to break (split into pieces)	šekastan	شکستن
to build (vt)	sāxtan	ساختن
to buy (purchase)	xarid kardan	خرید کردن
can (v aux)	tavānestan	توانستن
can (v aux)	tavānestan	توانستن
to cancel (call off)	laqv kardan	لغو کردن
to catch (vt)	gereftan	گرفتن
to change (vt)	avaz kardan	عوض کردن
to check (to examine)	barresi kardan	بررسی کردن
to choose (select)	entexāb kardan	انتخاب کردن
to clean up (tidy)	jam-o jur kardan	جمع و جورکردن
to close (vt)	bastan	بستن
to compare (vt)	moqāyse kardan	مقایسه کردن
to complain (vi, vt)	šekāyat kardan	شکایت کردن
to confirm (vt)	ta'yid kardan	تأیید کردن
to congratulate (vt)	tabrik goftan	تبریک گفتن
to cook (dinner)	poxtan	پختن
to copy (vt)	kopi kardan	کپی کردن
to cost (vt)	qeymat dāštan	قیمت داشتن
to count (add up)	šemordan	شمردن
to count on ...	hesāb kardan	حساب کردن
to create (vt)	ijād kardan	ایجاد کردن
to cry (weep)	gerye kardan	گریه کردن
to dance (vi, vt)	raqsidan	رقصیدن
to deceive (vi, vt)	farib dādan	فریب دادن
to decide (~ to do sth)	tasmim gereftan	تصمیم گرفتن
to delete (vt)	hazf kardan	حذف کردن
to demand (request firmly)	darxāst kardan	درخواست کردن
to deny (vt)	enkār kardan	انکار کردن
to depend on ...	vābaste budan	وابسته بودن
to despise (vt)	tahqir kardan	تحقیر کردن
to die (vi)	mordan	مردن
to dig (vt)	kandan	کندن
to disappear (vi)	nāpadid šodan	ناپدید شدن
to discuss (vt)	bahs kardan	بحث کردن
to disturb (vt)	mozāhem šodan	مزاحم شدن

29. Verbs. Part 2

to dive (vi)	širje raftan	شیرجه رفتن
to divorce (vi)	talāq gereftan	طلاق گرفتن
to do (vt)	anjām dādan	انجام دادن
to doubt (have doubts)	šok dāštan	شک داشتن
to drink (vi, vt)	nušidan	نوشیدن

to drop (let fall)	andāxtan	انداختن
to dry (clothes, hair)	xošk kardan	خشک کردن
to eat (vi, vt)	xordan	خوردن
to end (~ a relationship)	qatʻ kardan	قطع کردن
to excuse (forgive)	baxšidan	بخشیدن
to exist (vi)	vojud dāštan	وجود داشتن
to expect (foresee)	pišbini kardan	پیش بینی کردن
to explain (vt)	touzih dādan	توضیح دادن
to fall (vi)	oftādan	افتادن
to fight (street fight, etc.)	zad-o-xord kardan	زد و خورد کردن
to find (vt)	peydā kardan	پیدا کردن
to finish (vt)	be pāyān resāndan	به پایان رساندن
to fly (vi)	parvāz kardan	پرواز کردن
to forbid (vt)	mamnuʻ kardan	ممنوع کردن
to forget (vi, vt)	farāmuš kardan	فراموش کردن
to forgive (vt)	baxšidan	بخشیدن
to get tired	xaste šodan	خسته شدن
to give (vt)	dādan	دادن
to go (on foot)	raftan	رفتن
to hate (vt)	motenaffer budan	متنفر بودن
to have (vt)	dāštan	داشتن
to have breakfast	sobhāne xordan	صبحانه خوردن
to have dinner	šām xordan	شام خوردن
to have lunch	nāhār xordan	ناهار خوردن
to hear (vt)	šenidan	شنیدن
to help (vt)	komak kardan	کمک کردن
to hide (vt)	penhān kardan	پنهان کردن
to hope (vi, vt)	omid dāštan	امید داشتن
to hunt (vi, vt)	šekār kardan	شکار کردن
to hurry (vi)	ajale kardan	عجله کردن
to insist (vi, vt)	esrār kardan	اصرار کردن
to insult (vt)	towhin kardan	توهین کردن
to invite (vt)	daʻvat kardan	دعوت کردن
to joke (vi)	šuxi kardan	شوخی کردن
to keep (vt)	hefz kardan	حفظ کردن
to kill (vt)	koštan	کشتن
to know (sb)	šenāxtan	شناختن
to know (sth)	dānestan	دانستن
to like (I like …)	dust dāštan	دوست داشتن
to look at …	negāh kardan	نگاه کردن
to lose (umbrella, etc.)	gom kardan	گم کردن
to love (sb)	dust dāštan	دوست داشتن
to make a mistake	eštebāh kardan	اشتباه کردن
to meet (vi, vt)	molāqāt kardan	ملاقات کردن
to miss (school, etc.)	qāyeb budan	غایب بودن

30. Verbs. Part 3

to obey (vi, vt)	etā'at kardan	اطاعت کردن
to open (vt)	bāz kardan	باز کردن
to participate (vi)	šerekat kardan	شرکت کردن
to pay (vi, vt)	pardāxtan	پرداختن
to permit (vt)	ejāze dādan	اجازه دادن
to play (children)	bāzi kardan	بازی کردن
to pray (vi, vt)	do'ā kardan	دعا کردن
to promise (vt)	qowl dādan	قول دادن
to propose (vt)	pišnahād dādan	پیشنهاد دادن
to prove (vt)	esbāt kardan	اثبات کردن
to read (vi, vt)	xāndan	خواندن
to receive (vt)	gereftan	گرفتن
to rent (sth from sb)	ejāre kardan	اجاره کردن
to repeat (say again)	tekrār kardan	تکرار کردن
to reserve, to book	rezerv kardan	رزرو کردن
to run (vi)	davidan	دویدن
to save (rescue)	najāt dādan	نجات دادن
to say (~ thank you)	goftan	گفتن
to see (vt)	didan	دیدن
to sell (vt)	foruxtan	فروختن
to send (vt)	ferestādan	فرستادن
to shoot (vi)	tirandāzi kardan	تیراندازی کردن
to shout (vi)	faryād zadan	فریاد زدن
to show (vt)	nešān dādan	نشان دادن
to sign (document)	emzā kardan	امضا کردن
to sing (vi)	xāndan	خواندن
to sit down (vi)	nešastan	نشستن
to smile (vi)	labxand zadan	لبخند زدن
to speak (vi, vt)	harf zadan	حرف زدن
to steal (money, etc.)	dozdidan	دزدیدن
to stop (please ~ calling me)	bas kardan	بس کردن
to study (vt)	dars xāndan	درس خواندن
to swim (vi)	šenā kardan	شنا کردن
to take (vt)	bardāštan	برداشتن
to talk to …	harf zadan bā	حرف زدن با
to tell (story, joke)	hekāyat kardan	حکایت کردن
to thank (vt)	tašakkor kardan	تشکر کردن
to think (vi, vt)	fekr kardan	فکر کردن
to translate (vt)	tarjome kardan	ترجمه کردن
to trust (vt)	etminān kardan	اطمینان کردن
to try (attempt)	talāš kardan	تلاش کردن

to turn (e.g., ~ left)	pičidan	پیچیدن
to turn off	xāmuš kardan	خاموش کردن
to turn on	rowšan kardan	روشن کردن
to understand (vt)	fahmidan	فهمیدن
to wait (vt)	montazer budan	منتظر بودن
to want (wish, desire)	xāstan	خواستن
to work (vi)	kār kardan	کار کردن
to write (vt)	neveštan	نوشتن

www.ingramcontent.com/pod-product-compliance
Lightning Source LLC
Chambersburg PA
CBHW060029050426
42448CB00012B/2914